My Emotions-
By Poetical Definition

Before you venture into what I think of as my poetic dairy I would like to introduce myself. This book is a Journal of my personal style of poems and diary entrees. I have always been obsessed with words. My name is one of creativity and often the source of a good laugh, yet I love it for both those reasons and more. But we will get to my name later.

I am an African, born and raised in America. I was blessed with two culturally educated parents, One Christian and one Muslim. A large portion of my education was learned from being on the streets of Brooklyn, New York. I was *a girl* who was never afraid to speak my mind but I didn't know the beauty that lied within me.
I was *the girl* who would fight the world if it offended me. I would rather die than to admit I was wrong. I was *a girl* who fell in love with the worst, broke the hearts of the best. I experienced pains that I thought were going to kill me. It felt like my heart was trying to eat its way out of my chest. I was *the girl* who did everything in my power to prove myself to people who couldn't care less. I was *the girl* who almost forgot how to laugh. I was always *the girl* who learned how to take my pain and strife and turn it into an epic. I learned to take the moments I wanted to relive over and over, and turn them into sonnets.

When something makes me smile I grab a pen, when I feel confused I grab a pen, when I feel hurt.. I grab a drink, curse a little.. Then finally I grab a pen... and I write. I write until I understand, I write until I feel complete. I write until I feel cleansed. But I was selfish all these years. I was writing for myself, healing myself and enlightening.. Me and only me. Then I witnessed with my own eyes, my small poem fix someone else's broken heart. Proudest moment of my life.

I have been working on this book since I was 12 years old. I wish I could say it's finally ready but it's not. Life will always give me something to write about and I love the lessons I learn. So finally I am ready to release my first born into the world. I am still in the process of understanding life, yet it gives me much to write about. I was terrified about what people would think of me after this exposing book thus I kept it to myself for more years than I care to admit.

Finally I remembered a little chocolate girl who would kiss each poem she completed and smile with delight. I am in love with words and all the limitless things they can do. I have finally learned that it isn't what people think of you it's what they know of you to be true. This is what is true about me. I have loved, I have cried, I have learned, I have lost, yet I have continued to laugh. I have prayed on the things in my life that hurt me the most and honestly they hurt no more. I am sharing my work with the hope that it will help others relate, release and revive. Some of these works I wrote with tears in my eyes and an unsteady hand. Yet when the tears dried and i read my own words I felt stronger from it. I also want to give air to those who are feeling so buried by life's drama you can't breathe. We are all connected by our experiences. We walk the same roads in different shoes; some are more comfortable or colorful than others. But we must all keep going forward.

We all cry and laugh, and hopefully we live to tell our story. This is mine, but it's probably yours too!

Regardless of age, sex, race and cultural up bringing we all must feel. M.E. is just two letters that make up the title My Emotions, but it's not strictly about me. It's about all people and all emotions that life continues to expose us to. These are lessons we hate to learn and yet we are grateful for later. In the end I am just like you and you are exactly like me. I was once *that girl* who composed her poems secretly then locked them away with no intention on sharing them. Today I am the woman who educated the little girl. I learned this is not a secret hobby but a gift for healing. My words do not belong hidden in a shoe box under my bed but written across the skies for all to see. My story should be shouted so others may tell their story and help those who weren't fortunate enough to learn these lessons the hard way. Learning the hard way is the only way to make the lesson stick! This book gave me light in places where there were no windows or doors. I am sharing it with you because we all need some sunshine to make the rain go away, and stay away. I was once *that little girl* and now *that girl* has grown to become the woman in M.E.

As for my name, I am Saduda Oyo and this is my first book of poetry. Allow it to heal for you what it healed for me.

My emotions in poetical definition.
Introduction.
Poem-My Emotions.
Chapter One- Get out of my head!
1. Sometimes.
2. The Era(error)of us.
3. Please
4. Heart-Broken?
5. He's not you.
6. Ghost.
7. Brain Game The collections
   - Scene one
   - Scene two
   - Scene three
   - Interlude
   - Scene four
   - Scene five
   - The Retreat.

Understanding- Get out of my head.

Chapter Two- Here we go again.
8. Again
9. Re-run.
10. Eclipsed
11. Pitiful.
12. Stupid me.
13. Change.
14. Nobody's Somebody.
15. Last poem.

Understanding- Here we go again

Chapter three- Me Vs. You.

16. I don't wanna make up!
17. The battle.
18. Good day sir!
19. Twenty-Four-Seven
20. I hate you!
21. I do (female side)
22. I do ..me too (males side)

Understanding- Me vs You!

Chapter four- And now, I smile.

23. Rain and then
24. You
25. Smile
26. Joy
27. Thoughtful
28. Twilight.
29. Simple love
30. Oxygen
31. Crazy! Stupid! Beautiful!

Understanding- And now, I smile!

Chapter Five- Love that never dies.

32. Even though.
33. If I
34. Honesty.
35. Drunken words, speak sober mind
36. Tru
37. Contempt
38. Dear dairy I still love him. (journal entry)

Intermission –Truth Serum

- Truth Serum
- Journal entry # 14
- Journal entry #15

Chapter six- Know thy self!

39. Saduda
40. Just Me.
41. Reality
42. 1984
43. M.E.
44. Not Juliet.
45. Things
46. Bastard Child.
47. That Girl.

Understanding –Know thy self.

Chapter seven- Saved!

48. Lost
49. He,who makes me.
50. True love poem.
51. Invisible.
52. Life 101

Understanding- Saved.

Chapter eight- Somebody had to say it!

53. Pointless
54. Bipolar
55. You win!

56. Never ever after.
57. The ex
58. Just her, not me.
59. Life lesson 13
60. Life lesson 21
61. Life lesson 26
62. Dear Dreamer

Understanding –Life's Lessons

Chapter Nine- Memory Lane

63. Something's Missing
64. Ghetto Fairytale
65. Bitter Taste
66. The Night
67. The Human Violin
68. Broken
69. Downfall
70. I'd Rather
71. History

Understanding Memory Lane
Dedication

72. Family Affair
73. Writers Block

Thank you!!

My Emotions

It has come to my attention
That hearts eventually get broken
Opinions are completely useless
If the words are never spoken.
Introduction to my emotions
People are programmed
Feelings can easily be downloaded
All pouring out slowly
10 minutes before new ones are uploaded.
Tears dry and eyes breathe
Hearts mend
And true loves... tend to leave.
There is no prediction
For the unpredictable
Contempt with what it presents
Thus the disappointment is
Acceptable.
This is the introduction to my emotions.
Scathes on knees, elbows and even souls.
Braced for disaster
Thus, always startled when happiness unfolds.
Seeking comfort within fables and fairytales
Believing in mystical creatures, easier than facing the cold.
Holding your breath daily..
Since no one told you it's plausible to exhale
Still, devastated when ideas and perceptions
Fail.
This is the introduction to my emotions.
Eyes open.
Brain is ready to learn.
Memories are but vague visions
Of our valuable experiences.
So live in the now, accept your current reality
And let disappoints of the past
Crash and burn.

Chapter One: Get out of my head.

Sometimes
Sometimes I feel like I should cry
But my tears won't shake
Sometimes I miss you so much
I can actually hear my heart break
Sometimes I try
Sometimes I won't
Sometimes I love you
Sometimes I don't
Sometimes the pain makes me physically sick
Sometimes the memories fade away quick.
Sometimes I feel like I will be okay
Sometimes I don't want to live another day
Sometimes it hurts so bad I can't breathe
Sometimes I hate you for letting me leave.
Sometimes I wish none of this was true.
Sometimes I wish you were me and I was you
Sometimes I cry so long so hard
Even my vision feels dry.
Sometimes I wish you just ..still loved me
Who am I kidding?
Go back and Replace sometimes
 With all the time.

The Era (error) of us.
So it began
There was me
There was you
We met
We liked
And oh, the hell we went through.
Yet, we stayed.
And once again we loved
We laughed, we touched
We kissed, we hugged.

We bragged, we blushed
We looked too happy, maybe a little too much.
And oh.. the drama it brought
Still.. we loved
We laughed, but then we fought
We missed
We kissed
We made- up
We loved
We stayed...
Soon the rumors began, we denied but still we listened,
We ignored but somehow we listened again
Once more we fought, and stupidly took advice from 'friends'.
The very foundation of our trust began to shatter again.
We tried. Well I tried
We lost . Actually I lost
We loved , I think only I loved.
We cried ,no I'm sure only I cried
We end , I end.
I end. I end.

Please
I asked my heart to stop loving you
To my surprise, it denied my request.
So I continued to stay beside you
Hurting myself, like I did best.
I asked my eyes not to be so blind
They ignored me,
 Refusing to see all the wrong you committed
Continuously.
Only capable of seeing you loving me unconditionally,
But in actuality I was living naively.
Believing that if you didn't actually love me,
You would be noble enough to simply leave me.
I asked my body to reject your touch
It disobeyed me
Craving any part of you, daily.

I struggled to resist you,
Vainly.
I asked my mind to forget you, insanely.
Instead it replayed every memory, in a spiteful way.
Returning with two thoughts
For every single thought, I managed to push away.
Feeling hopeless that this was a fight I couldn't win,
I pleaded with my heart and made my request again.
This time re-evaluating what my plea could be missing
And it dawned on me why my heart hasn't been listening
A simple word that set me free from a lover's disease.
I humbled myself and asked once more; so embarrassed I forgot to
say it before
 I beg you heart to release this love,
For it is only, I who loves him and not he who loves me
So set me free from this pain.. Please.
There was one person keeping me here, someone I didn't expect to
see
I wasted time pleading with my heart, but all the while that person
was me.

Heart –broken?
Should I hate you?
Should I reminisce over everything you say and do?
Should I call you, and confess my true feelings?
Should I bash your name, as a form of healing?
Should I cry until my eyes are too dry to blink?
Should I depend on a substance?
Will the pain go away if I drink?
Should I attempt to move on?
Should I avoid playing our song?
Should I convince myself nothing we had was true?
Should I hate her for meaning so much to you?
Should I tear up your picture, throw rocks at you when you pass?
Should I tell my brothers to kick your ass?
I've tried everything, yet the thought of you still pains
How can they call it heart- broken?
If the breaking still remains?

He's not you.
The things he does
Reminds me of the things you'd never do.
The things he says makes me miss talking to you.
His style, a painful reminder
His smile, my misery finder.
Women call me lucky
For receiving such a man.
I'd explain my regret but they'd never understand.
 I had everything! The laughter, the joy.
The best friend all the perfect alloy
Late night calls will never be the same
Because every time the phone rings all I hear is your name.
 I am overwhelmed, drowning in my own depression
Missing you gravely
Feeding my own obsession
I should be over it by now
But I am not
Because every time he tries to get closer
I tell him to stop
I look into his eyes, sadly wishing he was you
I have run out of excuses,
I can no longer pretend
Nor will I try to.
No longer ignore the feelings I deny.
I want to move on, I swear I really do
But every time I meet someone special
I remember
He's not you.

Ghost.
I feel you here
But I can't see you
I'm wondering.. if I am talking to myself
Or is there a demon pretending to be you?

It's cold in here, I can see my breath.
I don't feel you anymore, I think you've left.
Am I being haunted?
By what is only left of you
Are you here now?
Or was that a just breeze blowing through.
I see something moving
are you doing that.
Did you leave this here?
Maybe I just forget to put it back.
I feel nothing now
Numb to everything beautiful I once knew,
Floating in love's limbo, trapped in our past,
unable to break free from you..
I can hear a heart beating, the pulse a little less steady than before
Feeling so far from reality, not sure if I'm even real.. anymore.
Can you even hear me at all?
The silence is so loud again, the loneliness has replaced my fear
Please.. Say something ...move a penny,
just show me you're still here.
Did you already leave me?
The house feels empty again.
How chilling how my ghost is not actually a ghost
But my living, breathing boyfriend.

Brain Game the collection:

Scene one.
You hurt me and yet I love you more.
I feel the tears
It's the pain I ignore.
If I could get you to show love to me
It would be only by accident or luck.
So if there is an inner voice trying to reach me?
Please, please speak up!

Scene two.

M.E.   12

Maybe you've said you love me
But my mind wasn't there.
I'd tell you how much I need you
But I doubt you really care.
A love so infatuating
Is something one should fear.
But since you set up camp in my heart
There is no room for reason anywhere.

Scene three.
Numerous times my brain has tried to kill you.
But my heart seems to keep you alive
Countless attempts to rid myself of you
Yet somehow you always survive.
Now with my brain on holiday
I am too stupid to leave you.
You'd think my heart would realize
You don't actually want me to stay.
Is it my imagination or do you keep pushing me away?

(The interlude.)
Minutes turn into hours
Tear drops turn into flowers
Days turn into years
And flowers turn back into tears.

Scene four.
The line between love and hate
Is quickly beginning to fade.
My heart you've already conquered
It's my brain you plan to invade.
I'd speak
But no one would ever hear a word I'd say
I've cried for you to cease
But you continuously hurt me anyway.

Scene five- closing arguments
I've given you my heart

Hoping you would release my soul
I've given you my life
Even though I feared
You'd leave my body cold.
I know what I want to say
But the words won't give.
My heart misses you gravely
It's the mind that won't forgive.
Loves un-conditional they say
And that I used to believe.
Truth is.. I would love you forever.
But my mind is home now
So understand this is why I must leave.

The Retreat.
Fret not fragile lover
I shall release you from your pain
The day is brighter now
You've won the brain game!
But be steadfast in love
For I shall return again...

Get out of my head!!!

These poems weren't exactly written to share. I was honestly bargaining with my heart to stop loving someone who was completely wrong for my well-being. This is another fight in the endless battle between the heart and the mind. The two of them rarely ever work as a team but still one cannot function without the other. The heart is always feeling and the mind always thinking. Since they are both trapped inside the same person this makes for one dysfunctional family! The heart wants to feel love regardless of the thoughts the mind keep pushing through. People spend so much time in relationships when they are unhappy that soon they begin to lose sight of why they are in the relationship in the first place. I was one of those people. And I am proud! Yes proud to admit I was in an unhealthy relationship many times in my life.

Like most people in love…we reach a point when it's either all or nothing. All meaning- Love this person forever and give them all of you. Normally this would mean you are happy with this person in a healthy relationship. Or at least one with two people on the same level of respect, with the same understanding of what is acceptable in the relationship. This doesn't mean that its perfect but it means it's livable with more happiness than pain and suffering. So giving your all isn't a job, it comes naturally. When a person decides to give nothing – it means exactly that and only that, you give nothing. This isn't easy; oh my God it's really one of the hardest things in the world to do. Giving nothing is also saying walking away from a situation you know deep down isn't right. When you know you deserve better and feel unhappy the majority of the time, the relationship is nearing its end. You are always looking for an exit or an escape, yet you make excuses to stay with that person. It can be abusive mentally, physically and emotionally, yet you will find ways to blame yourself. You spend the most of your days in the situation either waiting for your mate to return or waiting for them answer your ignored calls. You feel ignored and your mate spends little to no time actually with you. In fact it feels like they rather be away from you than actually with you! Or on the other hand you're waiting for them to leave so you can finally relax. Their presence is a burden, and you're always happier when they are gone. They are suffocating you and being needy. You go numb and simply go through the motions. This is unacceptable.

You find a part of yourself that keeps telling you to leave! Leave this person! Get out of their space or get them out of yours. Make room for someone new. Usually this occurs after two people have reached a point where they barely get along with each other, but try to stay together for all the wrong reasons. Either they live together and don't want to go separate ways for financial reasons, children, or the one most commonly used fear of being alone. They argue nonstop, live in a love less relationship, filled with infidelities, secrets and lies. This is damaging to you and all the people around you. You don't know it or maybe you don't care but you are teaching your children, it is acceptable to stay somewhere where you are not happy or even respected. Training them that it's acceptable to allow a person to abuse you and take advantage of you. We all were witness to the relationships our parents were engaged in. And look how it affected us.

Take a moment and think back to the things you remember, and now compare that to your relationships. We watched the treatment our parents accepted and it echoes in our lives. So why would you want to set such a low standard for your child? Or even worse for yourself? You're basically saying out loud that you rather be completely miserable than single. Really?? That's pathetic! Take 10 seconds and think about how your mate treats you. If you are in that dead end, worthless, painfully lonely, ugly ass excuse for a relationship; well consider this a slap in the face!!! Soon you become nothing because you accept anything. Anything!

When you decide this person isn't good for both y our life or your health, it's beautiful! Embrace the reality that your deserve better, that you aren't where you would like to be. Now you can find something that is worthy of you. You can truly be happy! At first you will miss the relationship because it was comfortable or convenient. Even though it had no long term potential to survive, it was easier than getting up and finding something better. Because that my friend is a job.

Walking away is one of the most trying and emotionally exhausting points in your life. This is where it gets hard. **The walking away!!!**

Okay so you decided that you are unhappy and you see now you deserve a chance to find happiness, CONGRATULATIONS you are already 5 steps in the right direction. There are so many ways to be freed from an unhealthy relationship but the easiest and most fruitful way is simple. FOCUS ON YOU! Focus on your life, your dreams and your goals. Focus on your own long term success. The things you want out of life. Be selfish! Be self-involved in the best way. Focus on making yourself a better more marketable person. Stop trying so hard to be part of a relationship and become part of yourself first.

Get out and go be happy, because happiness is not going to come knocking door to door to find you. And the longer you go without it the harder it's going to be to recognize it when you do find it!! Trust me, I learned the hard way, twice.

Chapter two: Here we go again

Again.
Here I am again
Again...
I went from your friend, to your lover,
From your lover back to your distant friend.
Recycled and remodeled
I stand here
boggled.
Again I've washed my face
Once more cleaned my hands
Yet I keep finding myself feeling dirty... in love again.
How is it that he keeps pulling me in,
It's my constant return I just don't understand.
So, here I am again.

Waiting for your words
To piece me back together.. Again!
Ironically these same words later rip me apart
Limb from limb.. Over and over and over ...again!
Your touch and your stare
Those nights of me waking up screaming your name
To find you are everywhere but here.
The winter ended
 The summer began,
We skipped spring, twice! And
Here I am falling.... again.

When he's approaching, my hearts beats faster
His love is too powerful, that bastard!
When will I ever break free?
How do I stand a chance?
Isn't love capable of lasting an eternity?
At this very moment he is taunting me
Keeping me dangling from his emotional string.
Giving me pieces of him , closer to nothing.
Do you love me enough to release me?

Years apart with the coldest of days in-between
I'm bleeding out in silence, why can't I scream
Feels like it is over
But I have been here before
Soon you will return to claim the remainder
Only to find there is nothing left anymore.
Relentless, you breathe into me
And place your heart in my hand
I open my eyes despite the tears
And here I am falling in love again.
And again.

Re-run
Too many times before
I've seen this show
This is the worst episode
The one when he decides to go
I'd turn away, but it always ends the same
She's ignoring him now, afraid to hear him explain
It's the scene with the explanation
That's when she finally breaks down
His lips are still moving but she doesn't hear a sound
I've seen this show
Too many times before
 I'm tired of this scene
And I don't want to watch it anymore.
I rewind back
When the happiness was still there
When she did nothing but smile
And he wouldn't think of going anywhere
Shhh..
It's my favorite part
When he opens up, and speaks from his heart
It's the reason I watch the show
I hoped they'd wed.
I hold back my own tears
And listen as he says
 I love you now

I loved you then
And after I love you forever
I want to love you all over again.
The re-run is over
But I think I'll watch that scene again.

Eclipsed memory
Musical notes revive emotions
I thought I lost
Jagged images yet vivid thoughts
Your presence travels through me
Pulsating, while burning vigorously
An Essence of you enters my room
I feel it floating directly above me,
I reach out, but it vanishes too soon
Your laugh, your sign,
Your touch....my cry..
My Cry? Is that the reason we said goodbye?
Fading Pictures of days spent,
Painful, Beautiful days
I think I remember..
I swear I want to remember!
But for some reason, my mind or my heart
Won't let the memories enter
Maybe.. I don't need to see.
It's possible my brain is only trying to protect me.
But I want to see!!
Do I want to see, this lost memory of what we used to be.
Would it destroy me? What makes it so scary?
But those flashes of you.
Oh how they make me feel..
And feel, and feel
I get so emotionally high, too high, I can't come down...
a high I don't want to release, why are we so bond.
It's as if I am walking in a dream, I can almost taste you
Is it real? Am I real, were.. we.. real?
WHY CANT I REMEMBER?!

What a love it was
Oh if the stories could be told,
every adventure, every giggle
All the passion they hold
I was happy.
So very, very happy.
I was loved
So very very loved
He loved me, didn't he?
But. Who? When and where is he?
I resume, the high slowly fades.
I can remember a love that devastated me
I prayed that I would forget him.. completely
I gave so much of me, that he left me utterly empty
I recall dry eyes, quivering hands
Numerous listening ears, either no one cares
Or they don't understand
I remember empty rooms, and blank walls
Neglected pleas, and ignored calls
I remember a love so vast
A love so true,
I remember becoming erratic
And completely consumed.
I remember the cold, feeling so cold, colder than ever before..
 I remember being alone so long;
 I didn't know who I was anymore.
I hear musical notes playing...reminding me
 It was I who prayed to forget.
Be careful what you ask for, sometimes you won't like what get.

Pitiful
Pitiful, it really is
For me to believe I could ever be his.
For me to stay around waiting,
Patiently may I add?
For him to come running to me,
Now I just feel sad.

Open arms?
Not a chance.
No roses, no poems or love letters
No romance.
I gave all I have
And some I even borrowed.
Like my heart, my time
And that pride I swallowed
I am ashamed of myself
For listening to the lies.
For desperately throwing myself
At one of those type of guys.
I thought I was smarter than this
But after that kiss
I lost all my intelligence
I am shameful
For allowing myself
To lose myself
For someone else.
Love for me is jagged now
Cutting me deeply, as I spin aimlessly around.
Pitiful, for me
To experience such a moral blunder
To ever let a man, who is not a man
Put me so far asunder.
And now I am dirty
And shameful may I add
Still praying that *myself* will forgive *me*
For making me look so bad.
It's really too pitiful,
 Too even be sad.

Stupid me!
I thought you loved me
I thought the person you were, was the person I see.
I thought you wanted to see me happy
I thought this was built on honesty.
I thought you made a promise to me.

I thought you'd never bring me misery.
I thought our love was true
I thought there was nothing we couldn't get through.
I thought nothing could take me away from you.
I thought the feelings were all mutual.
I thought you'd never make me cry.
I thought you'd never tell a lie
I thought we'd never say goodbye.
I thought a lot of things
That didn't turn out to be true
I thought I was safe with loving you
I thought this love was meant to be forever
I thought everything was perfect if we were together.
I thought you cared about me
I thought you couldn't live without me
I thought I was the only one for you.
Well....
Stupid, Stupid, STUPID ME!!
For ever thinking you could love me.
The way I ignorantly loved you.

Change.
The sun has set.
But you! (My love)
You're not home yet.
The snow has melted
The leaves have grown
The moon is whole again.
But you (my love)
You're still not home.
Over time all things change
And the old start over new.
Well in you're absences
I've changed myself,
Change myself from waiting on you.

Nobody's Somebody.
Nobody never loved her.

But Somebody always loved him.
Somebody kept trying to get through
But Nobody would never let her in.
Nobody never said the words
But Somebody heard them in her own way.
Somebody would never admit it,
But she knew Nobody never wanted to stay.
Nobody showed the signs, but Somebody refused to see.
Everybody knew the truth
Everybody except somebody.
Suddenly one day
Nobody was at home.
Gradually Somebody noticed she had always been alone.
Nobody never loved her.
But Somebody will always love him.
Relentlessly Somebody kept trying to get through
But Nobody never let her in.
Nobody should never stay where they don't want to be.
If you're nobody, then who would that make me?

Last poem
No more words to say
No more tears to cry
Our love has ended
Goodbye. Goodbye.
The last poem
It will go in our history
We lived an epic at the least
Simply rewrite fairytales
Invert beauty to the beast
The last poem, ever written never to be released
No more pain left to express
No more arguments to digress
Not a single love poem comes to mind
We have reached our peak
And apparently run out of time.
The saga has ended
The revolution never began

This is the last poem
To a love i thought would never end...

Here we go again!

Round and round and round. That is the cycle love takes. It's a circle normally it will do a 360 sometimes 180. Regardless of how I would try and try to get off the ride I would be stuck on the merry-go-round. Every time I would find myself turning the door knob to leave, something or someone convinced me to stay. Most times I was convincing myself. On the occasion that I would leave, I would come back. I would break up and literally fall in love with a new version of the love I just left. Fighting the same fights and feeling the same pains. But that never stopped me from trying at love again. Falling in love was always my favorite part of love. Until I learned what real love is! When you fall in love you never imagine the ending you just float around in happiness, that is probably the point. As I experienced different levels of love I learned more about myself than I ever imagined. Also I learned that even the best things come to an end. The ending is not the hardest part in fact it is the events that lead to the end that break your heart. I remember being so in love that I completely denied the most obvious evidence. Like if it was a court case he would have pled guilty before I would admit he did it. I was blinded by love so badly that the pain became a part of the relationship. Hence why when it was ending I was still clinging to the idea that I could fix it. The harsh reality that something is too far gone to revive hurts the most. There are two people in a relationship at the least. Yes you will always have other players but the two MVP's are the ones that matter. One of you is going to fall out of love first. It's going to SUCK! For both of you. The one who falls out of love first is going to try to stay in it. They are doing this to avoid hurting the person they love but what they don't know is, they are hurting them even more by pretending to still be in love. Sad but true. Another point I was trying to make in the poem "Again" was the fact that you will be destine to stay in the same situation if you don't address the issues you are having. If you feel ignored by your lover, talk to them, you're not good at talking because they cut you off then write it out

M.E.   24

in a letter. Somehow, some way you need to relay the message of how you feel, and it must be uninterrupted. It's very difficult to express your feelings when someone is speaking over you, telling you how they feel instead of listening. I myself am guilty of this. While my mate would express himself I would already have a rebuttal. I was not good at listening to how he felt. In fact I was convinced that he was wrong about how he felt. Insane? I know! But it was because I was not listening. I am aware of this now, and soon learned there were multiple mistakes I was making in the relationship. I was one of two, we were both guilty of destroying the relationship. Something as simple as listening to one another for 3 minutes or more at a time could have saved us. He and I are friends now because we learned this lesson too late.

This will work in friendships and relationships alike. When a relationship is showing signs of a terminal illness don't freak out. If two people are willing to work together on the same task, there is hope. You ever notice the word ship in relationships and friendships? That's why the word ship is in friendships and relationships. Even when the friends break apart, or the relation ends, the word ship is still intact. *A buoyant vessel*! Because ships are not easily sunken, some part always stays afloat. Sometimes the love keeps floating, sometimes the friendship or in some cases the lust. There is often a lasting a connection between two people who once loved another. As it should be, because love is built to last an eternity, in whatever form it takes.

When dealing with matters of the heart we have to accept that things always get worse before they get better, but we and we alone have the right to try. In life we may or may not find people who are worth the fight, and if by the grace of God you find someone who is worth it then fight! Fight until you have nothing left, Give it everything you have, stay up late and talk it out. Dig into your issues, and don't ever go to bed angry. If you have found the person who understands on a level no one even knew existed. A person that treats you better than you deserve to be treated, and still believes its not enough. This is one of those cases where you should give it everything you can to save it.

But... if you see that there is no saving the relationship whatever form it comes in, then give yourself space from the person.

This is the first thing you should do before you make any permanent changes. It's a healthy way to figure out what you want to happen next.

No relationship or friendship is perfect because we as humans are imperfect by design. As I yo-yoed back and forth in and out of love with my mates I learned so much about true love. It will have ups and downs, lefts and rights, ins and outs. It will stress you out; piss you off, change your way of thinking all while driving you completely insane. But it will also force you to grow, and educate your heart in ways that nothing other than love can do. So yes this was here we go again and trust me we will all be down this road again. My newest favorite part of love is learning who I am when I am in love! The cycle of falling in love, struggling with love, defending love and falling in and out of love. The incomprehensible ability the heart has to heal and try again is marvelous. Or is it completely insane?

Part three: Me vs. you.

I don't wanna make up
I am exhausted with fighting
Fed up with trying
Tired of crying
I don't wanna make up.
I am sick of yelling.
Annoyed with eyes swelling
Aggravated from dwelling
I don't wanna make up.
I am ashamed of explaining
Done with complaining
Now I'm comfortable abstaining
I don't wanna make up.
I am tired of I am sorry
I am tired of I won't do it again.
I am tired of the lying
I am tired of hiding whatever this is from my best friend.
I am tired of forgiving you over and over again

Make up? with who?
I hate your voice
And I am sick of looking at you.
We have no future
Our past is my hell
I cry my eyes out and you simply watch me.. as they swell!
I have been your fool, convinced my heart you can change
Wasted years of my youth.
And you are still exactly the same.
You feed off my pain, you're a leech, and now i see
Convincing my friends I'm fine
While you stand there draining me.
While you stand there! Draining me!
My heart is exhausted;
I am done with resolutions
Finally its come to my attention
That not every equation
Has a positive solution.
So ask me again I beg you, please!
I really want you to hear me
So get off your knees.
I am never coming back ,no way, no how!
Excuse my excitement I've been waiting to tell you this for a while.
Hope you kept the receipt for Kay jewels
Cuz honey we are soo thruuu
I don't wanna make up
And incase u didn't get the memo...
Fuck you!

The battle.
 I've fought this battle
For as long as I can remember
From the hottest July
To the coldest December
I've waited so patiently
For you to hand your heart to me
Barely standing, and that precious day has yet to arrive

That's what amazes me,
How ? With all this suffering
Is our love still alive?
As for My treason!
I've denied your curiosity
I've faked your chivalry
I've watched you mangle my heart
Then barricade my integrity.
My bodies exhausted, why is my heart so limber
I've fought this battle for as long as I can remember.
I have banged on your heart,
my pleas barely causing a commotion
To no avail, I still await your nonexistent devotion
Attacking you with passion and the deepest of emotion.
I've been fighting this battle, even longer than I remember
From the hottest July to the coldest December
Now it appears there is nothing left I can do
Countless casualties.
My shields are down
my weapons are all useless against you
With my white flag up high
I reluctantly accept defeat.
Congratulations
You have shown victorious in this battle for your heart
Since Loving you hath made me weak.

Good day sir!
I don't need you anymore
my hearts okay now
so you can give back my smile
and take with you this frown.
I don't need the drama anymore
my life is better now
so leave the anger outside and keep the volume down
if you cant tell,
I'm ignoring you since i only have ears for happy sounds.
I can't see you anymore
my eyes are clean now

I took away the rose colored glasses
and I can see 20/20 now.
Don't feel bad for me
don't even remind yourself of me
don't worry ..please
because I am finally completely happy.
Some things set you free
others hold you back.
So I hereby cleanse myself of thee
and all the substance it lacked,
I don't need you anymore
Good day sir!
Just the thought of being rid of you makes me happy..err!
I would prolong this good bye only out of pity, but really what for
So be a gentleman and kindly leave my key at the door
I say good day, I bid you farewell
You are here by relived of my hearts duties, so please don't dwell
Your services are not welcome anymore
Move forward, good day sir!

Twenty – 4- seven.
I walked today. All day.
I saw you, and sadly looked away.
You seemed contempt,
with "us" no longer being "us".
Weather jealousy became envy,
Or love became mistrust.
I dreamt today. All day.
I saw you, and happily dreamt away.
The moments of being happy together,
Tempted me to get trapped in that place forever.
I cried today. All day.
I felt the tears one after another
each one reminding me we don't belong together
I thought today. All day.
You sat etched in my brain.
Returning. Again and again.

I reminisced today. All day.
I closed my eyes tight to forget you,
but when they are open, all I do is miss you.
Twenty four hours a day
and seven days of my week.
Internally, I am suffering forever…yet.
I'm still too prideful to speak.

I hate you.
I am broken
Lost and confused
I feel dirty and completely used.
I hate you!
But I love you so, so much more
Every time I try to forget you,
I find myself humbled at your door.
I hate you!
For all you put me through
For not still loving me
While I was still loving you
I hate you.
When I'm remembering all the fun we had
Watching you move on,
While I stand there looking sad.
I hate you!
For those nights you held me in my sleep,
Those poems you inspired, forcing me to dig deep
The pain you inflicted without even knowing
The way you claim to love me, with none of it actually showing
Oh how I hate you.
Because now, I am broken
Into so many pieces I can never be fixed
So many have tried to put me back together
But nothing ever sticks.
I am shattered completely for that,
I hate you!
This is entirely your fault!
Harming you in some way, is my only peaceful thought!

M.E.   30

I am terminal. I may never feel better
Because of the pain you caused
I may be broken forever..
So I need you to know,
If you take nothing else from what I said
Please let these three little words
Forever be etched in your head
I hate you..

I do.
Why should I stick around?
If I am no longer attracted to you?
Is this the best time to admit
 That I am engaged to someone new?
Yea we took vows, and lied before our families
That I would love you and you would love me.
We gave our word, to the lord above
Where you would lead and love
I also did the same,
But I promised to submit and respect
I did this in the lord's name.
That was assuming I'd have a real man as my spouse
Not a boy with female tendencies
Watching bad girls club on my couch.
How can I respect you, when I barely like you?
Your every word is a lie, and I swear if I was a man
 I'D FIGHT YOU!
Yet, here we are for better or worse
And you're still incapable of having a conversation
without threatening me first.
Do you take him for your husband?
I do
I know I said it
But that's when I thought our love was mutual
But now
I don't like your opinions
And I hate how you think
You are the reason I cry

I am the reason you drink
We don't get along
We never speak
You say I am too controlling
Maybe it's because you're too weak.
It's so ironic how this marriage thing all begins
Two people make a promise to stay together forever
And spend the rest of their lives playing pretend.
Make believe, with make believe kids
Make believe smiles and make believe friends
Why do we use the term ..I do
Something like, 'sure why not', or 'I'll do my best'
 Is better suited for what we go through.
Do you take her to be your wife?
Who knew that beautiful man at the altar
Would be the ugliest mistake in my life.
I hate sports, and you're bored by plays
Friends tell me I am the lucky one!
At least he stays?
Maybe because he still loves me,
or more likely he is just counting the days.
Are we wrong for each other, or is it me?
And I don't need another session with Dr. what's his name
To know we are both unhappy.
I look at my ring, when I remember to wear it
I don't ignore your calls; I just wish I couldn't hear it.
We never speak, so how can we ever agree.
I am annoyed by you,
And I am sure you hate me.
It's all hazy and really i can't remember why we got married
Do you?
I just recall, blah, blah, blah
I do!

I do...me too(the Husbands side)
I knew you were selfish, when I proposed
I should have left you then, I suppose
But I didn't, instead I took it all the way

I ignored your flirting, and the hateful things you would say.
You never cook and you barely clean
You smile a lot but most of the time you're mean!
Yeah, you got me drinking
Wondering when I said 'I do'
What was I thinking?
I remember my vows, because I said them with pride
You forgot yours, because it's impossible to remember a lie.
You hate sports but you love to play games
Like checking my phone, and randomly yelling out females names.
Every time I touch you, all I feel is ice.
Who is this demon and where is my wife?
We don't talk because you are too busy accusing
But you refuse the divorce, you're so confusing.
You stopped loving me, because I remember the day
You called out his name in your sleep
And that's way I stay away.
You blame me for everything, it's always my fault.
But you were cheating, even before we fought.
I never make you laugh, but I hear you laugh all the time
Remember you promised to give me your heart?
What's yours is mine?
I tend to chuckle
When I think about what you said
You love me unconditionally
And yet you refuse to give me … nuff said.
You call me names, and you're worst on Sunday
How can someone so Holy, say the things you say.
You never dress up, and yea you're getting fat
Whining and complaining all day, who wants to come home to that.
"You don't even notice when I get my hair done"
No I am too busy noticing, that your co-worker looks just like our son.
Do you think this relationship was mistake?
I do.
And my mother, you are right she never liked you
Just like your friends don't like me
I pay all the bills in this damn house
And they sit on my couch rolling their eyes at me!

You quit your job to stay home with our Son , Jamire?
Yet somehow, I'm still spending money on daycare.
Your just like you mother, well that was out of spite
That was locking me out just the other night
You're no longer attracted to me?
Did I mention you went to a size 12 from a size 3?
You never work out,
But you always dress like at the gym
And please stop calling it baby weight,
Our son is seven
The therapist said we should role play,
But I wouldn't be able to face myself
If I had to say the things you say.
You used to be a lot of things before we got married
Where is the girl who I shared wedding cake with?
Where is the girl I carried?
I would send you flowers, but you are never home.
I would surprise you on my lunch break
But I am sure you are not alone.
I have been trying to keep us together
I signed up for therapy, to try and understand you
Now with the truth on the table, I can't believe I married you.
Would you take her as your ex wife?
I do.
I always thought you were unhappy
Finally I can say with no regret
Me too.

Me Vs You.

*Wow, Love can get ugly sometimes. I honestly wrote these thinking
that I would feel this way forever!! There were days when I was in the
relationship thinking, "how the Fudge do I get out of here?" Days where
I became someone I'm not! Days where I wanted my boyfriend to fall
down some steps simply so he could call out to me and I could turn my
back on him. In my defense that is what I felt he was doing with my
love. Yes things between us were this bad. There are before, after and*

during versions of my love within this section of poems. I laugh at some of them now, but during the time I was miserable.

These poems are not just about how painful a relationship can be, but also how you look or sound when you are choosing to stay in a dysfunctional relationship.

The scars you receive when you leave it and how visible are those scars will be in your next relationship. You learn so much in love about yourself but you probably don't apply any of it to your life until it's too late. But within those lovers spats your truest deepest darkest feelings are hidden between those harsh and insulting words. Due to a lack of communication you don't get to talk about them properly so they don't come out right, instead they eat their way out of you. You remind the other person of all the wrong they have done or have been done to them. All the knowledge you have of all the mistakes made in their life thrown into their faces....burrrrr!!! A very cold and hateful attack and we toss them like pillows.

When I wrote these poems I had reached the point where I had tried everything in my power to leave this person alone and for some reason I kept failing and finding myself right back in their space. The crazy part is, it wasn't him who was persuading me to stay it was me who was persuading him. In fact at times it seemed that he was contempt with us being over and I wasn't. I was chasing my own pain. What? That sounds insane why would I do that?

Because sometimes we run from one pain and run towards another. What I mean is sometimes we are so afraid to be alone we rather be anything but alone. Miserable, unhappy, and even abused. Anything but alone!! I remember being cheated on so much that I created a collection of females names in my phone so when my boyfriend went on one of his mini vacations (mia) I could call each one and find out where he was! WTF!! What the hell was I doing? A sane mind would have just walked away, changed the locks and started trying to get back to normal. But when I was that deep in love I was far from sane and Years from normal. I was disgusted with the idea of being alone, so much so, I stayed somewhere destructive for way too long. I admit that I used to be broken in that way,

Sometimes I might still be that way when too deep in love. The point is it's so unhealthy it's deadly. I am just sorry I learned this life lesson so late in love. But it's not too late. I am still capable of loving and trusting, even better I have a really high threshold for pain, since I have been taking so much of it for so long.

I have been in relationships where I felt completely alone and still stayed in it, in a sick attempt to avoid actually being single. But good news! I found a way to get out and still be happy. In fact happier! I took it one day at a time and I watched my progress. I kept notes to myself and wrote him letters about how he made me feel but I never gave them to him. Yet when I wrote them I wrote them as if he was going to read them. I admit, I checked his phone but never told him what I had found i just wrote down my findings. The things I found? Whoa! There were no words to the pain I was in. It felt so horrible reading the things I found over and over. I kept torturing myself, until I found out that it wasn't him doing me wrong it was me allowing him to do me wrong. And why should he stop? What was I going to do? My threats meant nothing because I was still standing by his side even after all those previous years of him hurting me. I was an idiot! To even imagine he would change. Alot of things change, but none of those things are people! One day while we were out eating everything came crashing down on me. Trying to keep it all in had become too much to endure. When I got home i ran into the bathroom of our apartment and I broke down. This was one of the most emotional moments of my life, but served to be one of the most cleansing. I cried so hard. I sat on the floor cringing at his text messages ,emails and pictures, hell there were even videos!
I wondered if I had a daughter and she told me she was living like this what would I do? I would kill him and punish her for being so stupid. So why? Why was it okay for me to live my life like this?

It wasn't okay! Soon I deleted all the evidence and moved out. I left everything I owned and took what I could carry. Each day that I felt sad or lonely and wanted to call him I would talk to God. I would beg god to remove the love for him from my heart and educate my mind on what I deserve since clearly I didn't know. I stand here today stronger. I look at people in relationships that don't have a happy ending, and I try to convince them that there is a better way, 90% don't believe me and sometimes find out the hard way. There are those few who listen who I can tell you are living as close to a real life fairytale than any of us may ever know! After everything loving the wrong person has put me through it has made up for by enlightening me .

Now I am more aware, sometimes too aware. But since I decide to end the relationship instead of letting the relationship end me first, I can still fall in love. That is exactly what I plan to do fall in love again.. And again.

Part Three: and now ..I smile.

Rain...and then ....
I stand in the midst
The midst of the storm.
Rains and chilling winds
And yet I remain warm.
Pain is washed away
 As tears gradually subside
Lightening so white
Flames lit the sky
Beside me, whimpering trees
Quivering before the storm
Crying hysterically, when visibly nothing's wrong.
I float threw the misty fog,
Watched by the gray eyed clouds
I feel like I'm going deaf
The thundering is so loud.
Now I am so enchanted by the storm
I barely move
And there I see it;
Vast, beautiful and so very smooth.
Color so vivid and bright
I swear I've never seen anything
So amazing in my entire life.
A rainbow, it had suddenly appeared in the sky
So magical, I thought I was going to cry.
There was nothing but rain all around me
And you've shown through
So obviously
You are my rainbow
And I think you're beautiful.

You.
You are my laughter
You are my pain
You are my joy
You are my name
You are my future
You are my past
You are my shame
You are my class
You are my far
You are my near
You are my emotion
You are this tear
You are my thought
You are my dream
You are my heart
You..?
You are my everything.

Smile.
You loved me
In the days when nobody liked me.
You were perfect in ways, that only Gods might be.
You touched me in spots that..... Tickled me slightly.
You placed yourself in my dreams ,
Daily ,mid-day and even nightly.
You knew me in ways no one took time to see.
You gave me feelings like:
Beautiful, exhausted and happy.
You never tried to kiss me without asking politely
You'd enter a room and it lit up so brightly.
You'd tell me how much you missed me,
In a crowded room, quietly.
You spoke poetically but frankly.
Knowing you was a blessing in itself
I can't imagine feeling this complete with anyone else
I am thankful for everything,

Even the stupid things love made me do.
Because now every time that I smile
I'm only thinking of you.

Joy
There is nothing I want more
Than to see you happy
You can take everything I own
It means nothing to me
But when you smile
It is so much more than enough
Your joy is my escape
When the going gets rough.
I need nothing
As long as I have you
Whether you're asleep or wide awake
I'm just happy being near you.
You arrive and instantly brighten my day
As long as you are happy
Trust me baby, I will be okay.
Smile for me once
And I am high for hours
I never knew someone else's joy
Could have so much power
Don't hurt pretty baby
Because it actually hurts me
Don't look sad sweetie
Because it makes me un-happy
Don't frown gentle lover
You're just not meant to
Your pain for me is completely un-bearable
Besides that, your joy is breathtakingly beautiful.

Thought full
I think you're beautiful
I think you're fun
I think you're smart
I think you're dumb

I think you might be the one.
I think you keep my head full
With thoughts of only you.
Oh did I mention I think you're beautiful
I think you're lazy
I think you're smooth
I think you're crazy
I think you're rude.
I think you are everything to me
I think you're attitude is crappy
I think that now that you've filled
My head with thoughts of you
I think you make me truly happy.

Twilight
The instant attraction was like nothing
I've ever known before
Frightened me terribly but left me wanting more.
Your eyes beckoned me to a place
of passion and blissful endeavors
Me Corazon canta su nombre, my heart sings your name,
in a foreign way.
There must be a another lifetime where we've met before,
No way this first encounter could leave me feeling
so emotionally sore.
I felt completely drawn to you
 The very moment you walked through that door.
Your lips called to me with such a beautiful allure
Me Corazon canta su nombre, my heart sings your name,
 in a foreign way
Something so new shouldn't feel so strong
This much longing is unnatural!
 so clearly it's wrong.
But when I close my eyes it's only your face I see
While I sleep I feel your hands caressing me,
Giving new meaning to the word.. Deeply.
If you say my name, my legs feel weak
Still, love at first sight is something so impossible to me!

Yet with everything I believe in, you are somehow all I need.
I feel you moving inside my brain, and when you're gone
 I can smell you all over my skin
Even from a distance you're penetrating my very existence
Over and over again.
You are the rhythm that makes music inside me.
Me Corazon canta su nombre, my heart sings your name,
 in a foreign way!
I can't be so smitten with something so new
But all I seem to be doing lately is waiting to hear from you.
So to make sense of this love that appeared over night
I must find this time capsule and make my reality right.
There is no way I could be so in love already
No way should his absence feel so wrong and heavy.
There must be a glitch in alternate reality
 Which brought me here to you
Maybe a time machine or magic was used.
It's possible that I've been brainwashed, or voodoo has been abused.
Maybe you hypnotized me and made me fall instantly for you
Those are all the explanations I have that sound close to plausible.
There is No way this is simply me being madly in love with you
That my friend is insanity!
And just seems way too.. Unusual.

Simple love.
I couldn't hear my heart before you
And now it's screaming
Living in a love so romantic
I still wait foolishly, for the credits to begin streaming.
Be still my heart
Come to me precious rain
Make four rights, and let's fall in love all over again.
Every day you're making my life appear surreal.
Move on rain, for pain.. I no longer feel.
You've placed a song in my heart
Which only seems to play when you are growing near
Suddenly ,I see no evil, I have no tears;

Your hearts rhythm is all i hear.
Your lyrics are movement for me,
Breathing essence into my soul,
While your very presence soothes me.
Shielded from harm, immune to cold.
Our love creates a concrete cage which barricades me
Irritating irrelevance deflected
Logic and reason evade me.
Everyday isn't always so perfect,
It's not always sunshine and white roses
There are those short moments, when we argue
 I die a little inside and watch the door as it closes.
But I quickly exhale and remember every day
He comes home and it's as if he proposes
I am plagued with the guilt of missing you while you dream
To be in your state of REM, I would give anything
I am grateful that regardless of how beautiful your dreams are
You somehow find your way back to reality, for me
You always awake with a smile, shining with the sun,
Just slightly more brightly.
You kiss me softly and squeeze me tightly
Your voice is the only thing capable
of preparing me for another day
I cherish you words, as I listen to you say.
"My lady, I always miss you while I sleep
Until I meet you again in my dreams,
Only agreeing to return to a reality where you are beside me,
So it's when I awake, and I see your face,
That I thank God for this simple love and pray
* He never removes me from this very place."*

Oxygen.
I have not taken another breath
Since we last spoke.
And every time I try to avoid thinking of you
I feel like your name is stuck in my throat.
Its love and that I hate to admit,

I thought I was done falling
But you're the one, and this.. this is it!
I am not exactly sure how I got in so deep
You are always on my mind while I'm awake
And I whisper your name while I sleep
Your thoughts are so valuable,
Your words are like air for me
It's obvious you are above this world
You're the only conundrum
that I want to remain mystery.
How arrogant of me to believe it would be so simple
A couple of letters, some pictures
 maybe even a visit or two
Now every thought that I have is either with or about you.
With that first spark, I knew I should flee
Unaware my desire to reconnect with you
 was more than congeniality.
Years before today I'd wished you belonged to me
The last time we were together I felt a growing chemistry,
Now I hear your voice and feel my heart skip a beat
I long for your love daily, and blush hysterically
 when we finally speak.
You are all I want, and truly you are all I need.
I feel complete just thinking of being with you.
I know you don't want to believe we are meant to be
So run as fast as you can from the idea of us
Because it's clearly too late for me
Your love is already my oxygen
Without you I would cease to be.

Crazy..stupid..beautiful!
For lack of better words he is
Crazy! Stupid! Beautiful!
Something odd and disturbing
Something simple, while distinctively unusual .
Something broken yet perfectly reconstructed
Some kind of symphony playing out of tune.
Still brilliantly conducted!!

So majestically he moves
So graceful, also
So arrogant and rude
So malice, but still so polite
why is this what I like?
Oh Mr. Crazy! Stupid! Beautiful!
I hope you're not insulted by how fond I am of you
Your childlike tendencies,
Trumped only by your very manly features
A fire between us breeding relentless sensual creators
Not an obsession I am proud of
Not one I 'm rushing to get rid of
Quite the contrary;
I'm intrigued with your flaws, and tickled by your vices.
Even though you're as high a risk,
as a teen with a new license.
Still, as you stand before me
 I'm turned on by each and every scar.
 Aroused completely by who you were versus who you are.
Curious about your story and yet
Bored by all those that came before me.
Annoyed by your intelligence, disgusted with your charms,
 Hate to see you flexing but i always feel
Completely safe and in your arms.
I look up and find myself submerged in a river
 That is your eyes.
Captivating me over and over, time after time,
Releasing me abruptly
Purposely dropping me flat on my behind
I recover and remember
Something so Crazy! Stupid! Beautiful!
Is far too complicated to exclusively to be just mine!

And now I smile!
It's hilarious to me that we work so hard for so long to get over a
person, and just as quickly fall back in love, sometimes blindly. But in
all honesty ..blind is the only way to fall. Its part of the thrill, and

exactly why we love falling in love. The hope that you will love again is a hard thing to destroy but it's possible to lose faith in love. We live everyday thinking about yesterday, or tomorrow. Most of us rarely get to live for today. The thoughts about past experiences can either haunt us or make us smile. We need love to survive. We need companionship overall so naturally our bodies will seek it, with or without our consent. I am honestly a very happy person, I have been through some things that have torn me apart and made me not want to love anymore. My faith in love has been shaken many times, hell it's been completely destroyed and somehow grown right back. This is our process. Fall part, get put back together. Fall down, get back up. Get your heart broken, move on and try again.. and again.. and again.

I am still here with a huge beating heart! Thank God!

If you know me you will say I smile very often, I smile a true smile; I don't know how to fake a smile. I guess because I don't want to know how. There is beauty all in this world and in the world after this. I notice things like flowers, trees, and fresh air and I admire them. God has created all these wonderful things for us to enjoy, to keep us happy. We must make an effort to be unhappy, hence the reason it takes more energy to frown than to smile. I will always believe in love regardless of how many times it knocks me down. I will always believe in helping others regardless of how many people take advantage of me. I will always trust people regardless of how many people stab me in the back. Because the world is still filled with simple beautiful things. But here is something to take notice of the next time the world is burning down around you, we can find happiness in the smallest dosages in the most unexpected places. Take a lesson from a flower; regardless of how many flowers have been ripped from its root, it still remains beautiful. In fact more flowers will grow in that exact place. Even in a flowers afterlife it's still beautiful, while it's sitting on someone's dining room table remember that flower is actually waiting to die. You thought your life was harsh.

       I have suffered; in fact we all have suffered but not every single moment of every single day. Life starts when the sun rises, and it starts over when the sun sets. Some people don't believe in God and that has nothing to do with me. There are some things in the world I don't want to understand. I rather just be happy that he lives in me. I rather just be grateful that God has placed his existence so loudly in my life I couldn't deny his presence if I tried. I smile because I have a relationship with God; He has always sent me signs to educate me. He has also directed me, even when I wasn't wise enough to know I was being directed he was still sending the message. I have been madly in love in my life with some very beautiful people, friends, family members and mates. I have experienced moments in my life that I will always be able to look back on and smile. I have had nights outside in the streets with nowhere to sleep, but found a park bench. Trying to stay awake with fear that someone was going to come harm me soon as I closed my eyes. I prayed the entire time that God would keep me safe and nothing happened! In fact I woke up to the sun shining on my face from actually having a serene dream. His blessings are large, some are small but they are always perfect. I have slept in my car in the winter with no money for gas, so I couldn't to move it or even use the heat. I have been jumped by a group of boys because I was just too brave!

We go through these things that hurt us so we can learn something important. That way we can avoid going through these situations over and over. When you are suffering do you just sit around waiting for someone to ride in on a white horse and rescue you, or do you get up and work your hardest to get yourself out of the situation. Start by talking to God and asking him what you should do next. He has different methods of communication for all of us.

You can be happy if you honestly want to be happy. You would need to exert energy towards moving forward. Thinking positively and smiling. Every day you have to get out and find your happiness, tap into your creativity, read new books and polish your skills. It helps to walk around and experience the world's beauty. I am not saying that every day you are supposed to be bouncing around, laughing at pointless things and smiling at random people. I am saying appreciate what the little you have and make your home or your space peaceful. If you need to paint or clean do so to make your space beautiful. My space is my bed. I don't have much, I have very little but I have my words. My words will feed me and one day help ease my family's suffering. I want to do so much to help people. I am currently homeless while I write this, I am living in an abandoned building, I have asthma and it's hard for me to breathe. There is so much dust. I go days without eating and I have lost a noticeable amount of weight. I have been looking for a job for months and been on many interviews, and I haven't received a word back yet. But everyday day I'm still out looking for work. I have cried so long for so many nights that I can actually smell my tears in my pillow. I have been through so much pain and watching people I love suffer hurts the most because I fell useless. I am a soft hearted person who often taps into the pain of others and take it on as my own. I used to think this was a curse but now I see it as a gift. I am supposed to go through this hard point in my life so I will not only understand what it feels like to have nothing but I will understand what hard work is all about. Saving money, being wiser in my decisions and how I spend my time. I needed to learn who I can count on and who I need by my side. So I will work the hardest I have ever worked in my life so will be successful and be able to help others. I will one day change the world. I will help so many people it will be unreal. I have nothing but 10 dollars to my name right now. I have no income coming in and I have a metro card from welfare to help me look for a job. I have two outfits to go job hunting and a resume. Right now I am smiling because I know that this situation I am in is making me a better more humbled person. I needed this!

I was ungrateful and took so many things for granted. When I first realized how bad my situation was I sat around for a couple of days completely depressed. Watching people I thought were my friends and family turns their backs on me. I felt helpless and I knew it was time to start changing. I was angry with them, but I had no right to be. Why would someone keep helping a person who won't help themselves? I was so sad and so scared I started making myself sick. I am finish feeling sorry for myself; I am done whining and complaining about what I don't have. I am only looking to the future for what I will have and what I will do. Positive thinking and speaking is the only way to move forward. To become productive you must first get up and start trying your hardest. Write down your goals over and over until you figure out how to get to them. Say things out loud that need to happen over and over. These words I write are all true and from my heart. I am happy and I haven't always been happy. I have accepted responsibility for my actions and my situation. I will be working on spreading my words so the world will know that we all suffer. We all cry, we all have had our hearts broken, we have all been hungry, we have all been poor, we have all been scared about where we would live or how we would eat. If you haven't well you have not lived! To suffer or struggle is to truly humble yourself. It forces you to appreciate.. Well everything! The truth is praying is becoming my food, my home and water. I pray that the hunger pains go away. I pray that I find a job and I pray that once this current state I am in is over, I never return to it. Because I am tired of suffering, I want to be able to help! still I am happy for everything I have because I can always have less. So talk to God and ask him to direct you in the direction he needs you to be. This is my direction and I am happy for it!

Part six: *love that never dies*

Even Though.
Even though our love has ended, time went on
The distance between us extended.
I love you still
Even though my heart has ceased to beat
And the ground has shattered from beneath my feet
As the world kept spinning and spinning and spinning.
I love you still
Even though the sky went black and the clouds began to form.
After the winter ended and I survived the storm.
I love you still
Even though you've shown me your back
And you've shut our door
And I've made a vow not to love you anymore.
I love you still.
Even though everyone sees the love you will never show
And I continuously claim to have let you go.
I love you still
Even though my heart has sealed itself shut, the breaking remains
My eyes sustain liquid form
And the memories inflict excruciating pain.
Even though since we last spoke
My heart hasn't continued to beating
Now my hand hurt so much from calling over and over
I think their bleeding.

Even though I analyzed the situation
And evaluated my brain
Acknowledged your absence.
And accepted the pain.
I've made a conscious decision
To love you forever
Even though, you've told me yourself
We will never be together.
I love you still.
I love you still.
I love you.. still.

If i....
If I could give you the world
It would already be yours.
If I could spoil you
I would buy you the all those stores.
If I could enrich your life
It would be a fantasy.
If I could make one wish
It would be to always see you happy.
If I could move the stars
They would spell your name.
If I could change the world
You would stay exactly the same.
If I could show you heaven
You'd see what it's like being with you.
If I could get into your subconscious
I'd make your dreams come true.
If I could erase your pain
I would cherish every day.
If I could travel your journey
I would leave today.
If I had a kingdom
I would give you my crown.
If I could carry your burdens
Your feet would never touch the ground.
If I could fight your battles

I would never scream defeat.
If I could shower you with presents
They'd always be at your feet.
If I could serve you like a king
It would be my honor.
If I could always protect you
I would be your armor.
But I must apologize
For I am only human.
I cannot grant any wishes
Or save the world from its ruin.
I cannot move the stars
Or change what you've been through.
I cannot grant you the impossible
Hence why I cannot stop loving you.
Yet, I would refuse
Even if I had the power to.
That is the one thing
I would never do for you.

Honesty
If I left you, I'd be back
If I said I didn't love you
It was an act
If you need me
I'll be here
If you're in pain
I would honestly care.
If I hurt you
It was a mistake
If you refused my heart
It would surely break
If you're lost
I'd find you
If you're wrong, we're wrong
Because I'm always behind you.
I'm behind you.
If you've doubted us , please don't

If I said I give up
Honestly I won't
No matter how long you're gone I always miss you
Forget all the games I've played and remember who I am
Because in all honestly
All I want from you is your hand
With honesty there is nothing we can't get through
So if you've loved me, truly?
Please continue.

Drunken words; speaks sober mind
For everything I am.
And everything I will never be.
For all the wrong I've done.
For all the wrong done to me.
For every day I cry.
And for every day you cry for me.
For every love I've known
and for every love that's ever known me.
There is no ending to no beginning
there is only you in my drunken haze.
The bottles empty, yet
the feeling stays
time will go on
love will start a new
but I will only love once
as I only love you.

TRU
When i was with you all my poetry seemed so surreal
Bizarre, how all the words i wrote
Was a slideshow of what you made me feel?
You inspired me in ways Plato would admire.
Not just lust, obsession and burning desire.
But love.. Oh love …. An entity one could never destroy.
The way an artist loves a fresh canvas

Or a mother loves her baby boy.
A magical thing that was beyond, lyrics or rhymes
A love that honestly frightened me at times.
You created beauty that i never knew before
And with those intermission in between,
I felt like i wasn't breathing anymore
A fairytale, thus in reality... Too good to be true
Still, every day I pray god makes many more just like you.
With your love you educated my heart
on what it was meant to do
This is why at first i was hesitant
Since, true love seemed so.. unusual.
But here i stand, drenched in an essence that is you
Poetry spewing from my pores, moons are full, skies are actually blue.
I assume by now you are blushing since you know it's directed at you
Please forgive me if i overdo it
I have a flare for the dramatics
But since this is your umpteenth poem
I figured you are used to it.
I 'm simply grateful for all the amazing things
You showed my heart it could do
I apologize for all the compliments
But when it's true, its tru!

Contempt
There is no denying
You know, that happiness we shared.
I am going to miss the moments
I'll try not to shed any tears.
I don't have to be your girl.
You can pretend I was just a crush.
We don't have to hold hands
We don't ever need to touch.

I never thought knowing you
Would be more than enough for me
There is no denying
That your friendship alone made me happy.

I am contempt
As long as we both remember
What we had wasn't fake
You were the only man
Who held my heart, so carefully
Making sure it wouldn't break

You don't have to belong to me
You don't have to try
You don't have to say the words
I know what you feel inside

All I need from you
You've given me that and so much more
You don't have to worry, it doesn't hurt anymore
Please remember, It's natural that I cry
We may never be married
And that hurts I won't lie.
But with everything we had
I couldn't ask for anymore
The memories will keep me contempt forever
Even though when reminiscing too long
I end up feeling sore.

Dear diary, I still love him.

Jan-21-2005 (4:39am)

I am hoping in time I will be fine. Sometimes I even think in rhythm.. I can't sleep, well obviously. Right now I am a little sad, well mostly I am confused. This love thing, is just so ..this is.. just so ugly. Love...damn when it's this strong it always hurts. It's just too strong and I have no control over the things being in love with him, makes me say or do. I say him because I am just tired of saying his name. I talk about him all day. I dream about him all night. You just get tired you know? Of saying it! HIM! HIS! AND HE!! Get out of my head!

What the hell about me! Me and my emotions, me? My thoughts about me? It's almost like my brain and my heart got into a fight over my heart loving him. So now my brain is mad at my heart for not being smart enough to leave him alone, currently they aren't speaking. Now my heart has taken complete control over my body and soul. Making me call him all day. Making me say things that make me look dumb. Loving him is so hard! Too hard. Now my brain is sitting up there rewinding old memories over and over. Just to up-set my heart, like pouring salt into those deep wounds. The wounds that weren't ever trying to heal. No, they rather just lay there open; Bleeding until there is no more left... I'm dry.

Since my heart is calling all the shots my brain is getting bored, so it brings me to my present state. Nothing left for my brain to do but think about him! So over and over my brain plays this movie of us in my head. And oh did I mention as it plays it burns? And burns and burns and after it burns, it burns some more. I watch as friends become lovers. Then as lovers become phony friends. I watch as phony friends while they deny emotions and attachments but give in to temptations; continuously. The tape ends but the saga continues.

The madness always made sense when they were together. The rain would dry, and the sky would seem so much brighter than ever before. I see the leading lady, in her most traumatizing role. There in her I see myself. That's when there is no more convincing myself I don't still love him. Denial is wonderful it got me this far. But now I can see I am on my own. You read about love, a love like this. Maybe you lived it, maybe you still do. If not let me define it. No boundaries, no borders, no rules, no limits, no safety ,no breaks. Just pure un-cut, un-tampered, UNCONDIATIONAL STUPID F***ING LOVE!

And you know what, you never see it coming. The truth is, I will never stop loving him. Even if I wanted to, which clearly I don't, I wouldn't even know how.

M.E.   54

Not that I have even tried..

Truth 101!

My life is nobody's fairytale regardless of how much I try to keep up appearances. There has been so much pain and betrayal in my life it hurts to admit it. I trusted in the wrong people time after time. I gave more of myself than I had and always felt cold afterwards. I have befriended people who knew they had no intentions on being a friend to me. I let people live in my home who did nothing but take advantage of me. I have slept in a car with no heat and no money in the winter. I have spent weeks wandering the streets because I had no place to go. I have been back stabbed and abandoned. I have cursed Gods name simply because there was no sign of love anywhere in sight for me. I regret that now. We tend to think that life is always over when they are suffering. So many times I have felt the same exact way. We hold their hand out and ask for things but never want to give a damn thing back. No one makes an effort to pay it forward and we sit around wondering why the world is in the shape it's in. So do we really wonder why it is this way, or is it just easier to pretend to be naive?

I am going to share a journal/diary entry with you now that may be darker that you had expected for a poetry book. Yet I am going to share it so that you the reader can feel how I felt and maybe it will shed light on your darkest moment. It's just a little easier to know someone is there with you. At least you know I am or was. I want you to know that these moments of depression and sadness pass. They vanish and happiness once more prevails. Pain is side effect of getting through something almost unbearable to survive. Congrats you are stronger than you thought! Suffering is never permanent but the strength that you gain and the lessons you learn are.

Journal entry #14
Wednesday December 5th 2007.
Where- no fucking place!

I am suffering!!!!!More now. Everything seems wrong in my life. No matter what I do or how hard I work. I can't win! My mother could care less about me. My father doesn't remember I exist. I have no one. No one I can count on. My boyfriend is selfish, my friends have their own lives to worry about my issues seem minor compared to their own; until they need someone to listen to their problems until then, I don't matter. No one thinks of me the way I think of them, and I can't change who I am. I can't change myself from always putting other people before myself, and look where it gets me!

Death. Lately that's all I seem to be thinking about. If things get any worse....i am going to take my own life. I have nothing to look forward to. No one is truly concerned about me in my life, no man, no guardian angel, no fairy god mother who is going to whisk in and save me. I was never lucky. I never felt blessed. I am on the other hand am getting used to suffering all the time. I watch as friends with real mothers, real fathers just live better lives. Depression is so real for me now. I feel like I am at my end.

So at this point I give up. If I just lay here and don't move and don't breathe I won't feel. I won't be hurting anymore because I wouldn't be here, and no one would care. I won't care about anything since no one cares about me.

I am not blessed! I keep hearing people say be blessed or how they are blessed, and I am dying to know what that even means. So people who are blessed don't suffer, hurt or even cry? Every time I am happy it is taken from me. My mother does nothing but talk down to me, STUPID, FAILURE, and FAT! EVERYTHING I DO IS SO WRONG!

No one loves Saduda, not even Saduda. Maybe this is my destiny to always be in pain. To always suffer, to remind others how lucky they are. Everyone with good jobs, good boyfriends, real parents. And homes! Why don't I have it? I am not even asking what I did anymore because if I did something so horrible that I am suffering like this wouldn't I remember?!

Oh my God, I am crying...me? I am fucking crying!! Ahhhhh! Today I am crying tears of failure. Defeat. Is it true is Saduda giving up on everything?

I can't even get to work , wow just another thing I can't do. I get a job and no transportation, peanut butter and never any jelly is the story of my life!

Why am I even living? You try and you try and try and still no good comes. People make promises to me, to help me and keep breaking them. I am not a thief, I never stole in my life, I am not evil or grimy, I don't deserve this! I don't!!!
Instead of people trying to help me they rather talk about me. wow.
I cant....................

Wow!!!Honestly I had forgotten how bad the pain was then. As I re-read my own words I fell pity for myself. I remember all the things that were going wrong in my life and how I felt like life was over for me. Like death was actually an option to soothe the pain. I mean come on that sounds like insanity just saying it. The truth is I cried so hard for two days after that. I came back to feeling stable two days later and wrote again...remember I am sharing this is all so something can be learned from it! So please don't judge me, and even if you do it doesn't matter because I already learned from it for myself.

Journal entry #15
Friday December 7th 2007.

    I am doing much better than the last time I wrote. I still have my two jobs and somehow I am still working towards my goals. I am learning what is important. It's essential to my survival in the world we live in. Hope. Hope is all I have for now and I am doing everything in my power to hold on to it. When you lose hope you lose your life. Because everything else just seems pointless when you have nothing to look forward to. When you lose hope to go forward, everything starts falling down, crashing around you and soon your days seem longer and darker. You need to find what's worth living for and hold on to it. Write it down and save it, paste it on walls around you. Do whatever you have to do to keep it in mind and in sight because if you lose it, life ends.
Mine is something I have felt in me all my life, I Saduda Oyo will one day change the world. People will hear my story and find peace. Sounds crazy but hey I'm still living, throughout everything I have survived it! Someone out there is rooting for me to succeed. Because of that little thought, because I have a destiny to fulfill, I didn't give up yet! **Suffering is only temporary***...I have been through so much pain*

lately I have been losing myself. I didn't remember the things that made me, me! So soul searching and some personal time should do it. I am determined to find the best version of Saduda Oyo and show her to the world! Because just as much as I need the world to exist to survive, the world needs Saduda to exist so it too can survive. I know that's reaching but it's a long way from how I was feeling a couple of days ago. So I say to you ROCK BOTTOM, I HAVE SEEN YOU AND I HAVE MOVED UP ABOVE YOU! YOU'RE NOT SO TOUGH! YOU LOOK A LOT SMALLER FROM UP HERE!

I'm making it short today because as always I gotta go to work, just wanted you to know I'm ok! ...ttyl till next time.

Thus begins the Journey to finding myself!

Know thy self!

Saduda

Slowly she steps
Swiftly she walks
Eventually she smiles
Intellectually she talks
Invading his mind..
Lyrics so unique
Whispering love spells
Poetry so deep.
Body of the devil
Eyes of a saint
She is everything
And yet she ain't...

Just Me
There is no Mr. Right
There is no perfect mate.
No soul mate or life mate.

Just me!
There is no perfect shape, no perfect face,
No perfection
Just me!
There is no secret,
No mystery, no makeup.
Nope.
Just me..
Dark and lovely
Simple, short and sweet.
Just me.

Reality
An endless funeral within my head
The oppressive lover, lying in my bed.
Quivering emotions tearing me apart
Tear-jerking love scene, continuously playing in my heart
Confused lost little girl.
Straightening hair that's meant to curl.
Bulimic life style, with effective results
The vomiting is toxic, but the denial helps.
Living vicariously through a fairies mystical pain
Beauty is tedious, so I won't complain!
Beckoning heart breakers, with inverted smiles.
Poisoning thy true self,
While plagiarizing styles
Frantic tears melting my face.
Wondering aimlessly, never finding my place.
Chasing my fabrication, I've named MR. Happy.
These are the piercing pains of my reality.
Sleep.
Wash. Rinse
Repeat.

1984
Dear God, It's me Saduda.
Do you remember the day I was born

what was the weather like?
Was it a beautiful day or was it pouring
Enough small talk, this is really about my mother.
Something's wrong lord, we don't get along with each other.
Did she seem happy Lord,
Did she smile or look kinda mean
Did she kiss me all over Lord
And promise me everything.
Did she hold me close to her at night
Did she pray for me to come out alright.
Was she happy to see me
Did she thank you lord when I came out healthy?
Did she sing to me Lord, tell me stories and Tales
I am asking lord, because that's not the way it feels.
Why is she so mean Lord, what did I do?
I am sorry for whatever it is, I swear I didn't mean to!
Was I ugly Lord, or not as pretty as she hoped I'd be?
Did I cry too much?
Is that the reason she never says she loves me?
Did she hate me Lord, when I kicked from within?
Did she ask for ten toes and fingers, over and over again?
Did she read to me Lord, or speak your name in my ear.
When she saw me for the first time,
What was she thinking Lord
What did you see in her mind.
When I fell down, did it hurt her more than me,
did she truly care? When I cried
Did she shed a tear.
In her heart Lord was there ever Love for me?
I am asking Lord, because from here I can't see.
Lord if you knew things would be this way
Why then Lord didn't you take me away.
Why did you let her keep me, when she treats me so cold ?
Am I required to help her lord, now, or when she is helpless and old
Why Lord? Was I placed in her life
when she causes all my pain, and inflicts all my strife?
I love her Lord, and I swear I try

M.E.

But she is the only person that can make me cry.
It hurts Lord to know, we are not
what a mother and daughter should be
I know there is a reason Lord,
but why her, and why me?
She doesn't like me lord
I don't think she ever did
Maybe we should go back to 1984
and just give her a better kid.

I was raised in a home that was far from perfect. Like most of us I blamed my mother for all the pain in my life. I was bitter because of the relationship between My mother and father, and sadly blamed it all on my mother. I learned of my mother's pain from family friends and family. She never let me know why she cried at night, or why she left my father. She never bashed his name in front of me or tried to keep me away from him. Instead she kept up appearances and gave me a fake smile to mask her pain. I don't know she was unhappy with my father I assumed it was something I was doing. My mother was miserable and couldn't show the affection I needed because her heart was broken.

The relationship between mother and daughter is extremely fragile. It is detrimental to everything the girl becomes in her adult life. If not natured properly, it can tarnish her womanhood completely. How often do you see a young girl or an older woman on the streets and shake your head is distain? Too often. It normally our first instinct to blame the mother. In some cases that is precisely the answer, but not in all. A mother's love is food for the child, this food decides how healthy the child will be. A mother in my opinion has the hardest job in the world. I watch as mothers struggle with strollers up and down steps and men push past them rather than help. As pregnant woman work 12 hour shifts at their full time jobs up until the point of labor. Mothers don't get sick days. They don't get time outs. They don't get "me time". I read my poem and I remember that while my mother was working a job she hates, living in a place she despised, and getting less than 6 hours a sleep a night I was complaining about the sneakers she brought me. It makes me grateful for one big thing; I didn't get me as a daughter. As children we forget how easy we had it, but when we grow up we remember we were ungrateful. So hug your mother, make her life as easy as possible, work extremely hard to make her proud of you because it's not fair that she worked a full time job for your whole life and didn't received any benefits. My mother and I were not as close as I would have liked us to be as I was growing up. It wasn't until I wrote this poem that I realized how much I need her approval and love. I love my mother more than I love anything in this world and I am grateful to her for making me the way she did. I am sorry I didn't understand that growing up, this poem was hard to share because I know what I know now. To Mommy, I'm sorry it took so long to see all you have done for me. Thank you for being so strong for so long, your beauty is timeless! I love you so much!

M.E.

If you stopped for one moment,
To look at me
You'd see a girl dying
To make you happy.
If you took one second to look back,
After we've said goodbye
You'd see the tears forming in my eyes.
If you tried just once to listen to me,
You'd hear all the things that make me pretty.
If you stopped and waited you would have seen
That without you.. My life doesn't mean anything
If you shut up just for a little while
You'd see the wonderful thing about me is my smile.
If you tried just a little to understand me
You'd see, that's it you that makes me crazy.
If you thought at any moment
That my love for you was a lie.
If you'd listen very closely
You would have heard me cry.

Not Juliet.
I want flowers but I don't want pain
I want to be in love
But I don't want to be heartbroken again.
I love a good romance but I don't want to cry at home
I am not Juliet, and sweetheart you are not Romeo
I'ma be real, when it comes to loving me
There is no such thing as half assing.
I want happiness in ways we only imagine
Winters on an island, summers in Paris.
Two kids and a house, somewhere with a beach
Something simple but tastefully unique.
I see your potential
I really do.
I know you are Loyal
And your heart is true.
I want a fairytale and I need it to come true.
But I am no Juliet and I'm not killing myself for you.
So this is who I am, and I already know you
We are not living in a story book
But we can do our best to.
Start with flowers
Speak with honesty
Make love with everything you got
And always be real with me.
But remember I am human
And I make mistakes
And I won't spend my days
 Bare fare in the kitchen baking cakes.
I'm bratty, spoiled, and kind of superficial.
Great in bed, clean, fun and very flexible.
So buy me shiny things
And I will hook up ya steaks
You take out the trash
And I'll dress up for our dates
Treat me like a princess

And I'll make you feel like a king.
Trust me, I'm still no Juliet
But I am everything and more
Romeo would dream.

Things.
There are things
Things you will never understand
Maybe it's because you're you.
Maybe it's because you're a man
Things that made who I am
But not who I chose to be
Things that make me cry
Things that make me un- happy.

Things that break me
Things that create me
Things that debate me then irritate me.
Things that make me smile
Things that drive me crazy
Things that make me mature
Things that make me act like a baby.

Things that make me strong
Things that make me mean
Things that make me laugh
Things that make me scream

These things didn't kill me
So they must make me stronger
Even though this things
Used to hurt like hell
These are things I got over!

Bastard child.
 It's funny how you made me
But you don't even know me

It's sad how you're supposed to love me
But you've yet to show me

It's crazy how little you care for me
Your selfish spoiled attitude
Has caused me nothing but hurt and misery.
It's still a mystery to me
How easily you've abandon me.

You filled me up with traumatizing memories
But always left me feeling empty
I am so tired of you disappointing me
That now I am on the floor
That way neither one of you
Will get the pleasure of
Letting me down anymore

Its odd how with time
Not much has changed
Except for age location
And last names

But please don't worry
I will heal in time
As long as I remind myself
It's your lost
I will be just fine.

That Girl.
I began to grease my skin this morning
Black, crispy, and chocolate
Magnificent and never boring.
I tried to comb my hair today.
Nappy, tangled and beautiful.
Broke four combs and I was on my way.
I squeezed into my jeans for about an hour
Huge, thick and voluminous
With a neck breaking power.

I glanced at the women in the mirror
You know that one I've seen many times before
Admired her beautifully full and luscious lips
Blew her a kiss and headed for the door.
I yelled to a *girl*
One I used to call a sista, I had to raise my voice
Or I would have missed her.
She used to be a different
Before she apparently lost her mind
Blue contacts, blonde hair
I assume she hates her kind.
She said her hairs too rough,
And didn't seem colorful enough
She said her eyes are boring
So blue ones should make the *boys* more adoring.
I smiled and sent blessings her way
Told her when you love who you are
You will be stunning on that day.
I caught a glimpse of the women
Who used to be a *girl*
Who loved contacts and processed hair
Hated when hers would curl.
Today her Body curved as if she felt rhythm beneath her feet
Women admired her complexion, as she glistened in the street.
Dark brown eyes that captured vision and true beauty
A heart dedicated to her people and her community
Skin kissed by the sun, smooth as a midnight pearl
I am fortunate to be black
I am grateful to no longer *be* that *girl.*

Know thy self

I didn't know who I was for so long, and each poem helped me get closer to the truth. The truth is, we spend so much time listening to what people think of us we lose who we are. So then since we are lost we allow people to tell us who we are, or should be. I didn't know how to be me because I didn't even know who I was. I struggled with one of the worst cases of an identity theft. Except they stole something that I was basically giving away! I hated myself, I hated my complicated name. I hated my dark skin. I spent years of my life with people telling me "YOU ARE SO PRETTY FOR A DARK SKIN GIRL!" I cannot express how much I hate to hear those words! I wish I could say I only heard them from people of a different ethnicity, but that would be a lie. I heard it most from people of my race and worse almost the same complexion as me! I grew up thinking there was something wrong with my dark skin. With all the negative reinforcements around me; it's no wonder so many girls bleach their skin. My brother called this the complexion complex. I suffered from this for 23 years. I hated being dark skinned for so long it's sad. Today, I love my skin; I brag about my skin, I put my beautiful dark skin on the cover for that reason! I blame myself for not loving me as much as I needed to be loved. In my defense I didn't even know ME, so how could I love ME? Now I am being quoted as loving myself too much, HA! As if there is such a thing!

I mean come on!! Who loves you if you don't love you? Would you buy a house if the previous owner of the house describes it as "miserable, ugly, too fat, too skinny, unattractive, boring, and a real loser?" I would hope no one would describe a house with such poor adjectives but you get the picture. We are conditioned to be unsatisfied. With today' standard of what is beautiful, and what we should all strive to look and sound like. When you reach a point in your life when you don't love the person staring back at you from the mirror then you begin adjust the person. You don't like your weight? Change your weight; you don't like your skin? Change your skin. You don't like your feet? Change your feet. Your hair, your eyes, and soon your very existence will be the final change. Let's be real, there will be always be something about yourself you don't find perfect.

So if you are constantly changing yourself based on who you find in the mirror. CHANGE THE DAMN MIRROR! If there is a person constantly trying to change you, CHANGE THE DAMN PERSON! Beauty is not a physical attribute it's a description. Normally used to describe something you find appealing in a positive way. Self-hatred and Self-mutilation are never beautiful. However, confidence seems to be one of the most attractive traits found in a person. When you look at a confident person take look at their body language and their attitude; feel their energy. The most appealing quality you can endow is self-confidence! Or you can change all the things you find less appealing for as long as you like, but always know those changes with never stop. You don't want to be 70 years old afraid to leave the house without make up, do you? Love begins internally..

It's a battle that you fight within yourself until you make a truce with your inner beauty. The moment you find that person inside you who is, fun, loving, thoughtful, honest, creative ,original. Loud, quite, emotional, strong, weak and everything wonderful and awful about being a human being, you will find true love for yourself. There was a point in my life when I was homeless, hungry, starving, depressed, scared and completely miserable. A point where every new day felt like a curse. No laughter, no reason to smile and absolutely no happiness. There was a reoccurring darkness that I simply could not escape. I 'm grateful i captured those moments when i felt like the world was over and there was nothing left to live for. . I wrote a collection of poems in those times. They now serve as motivation! I've turned my pain into uplifting stories of triumph. So when i look at my past pain I simply smile because in time all wounds heal. The sun always seems to come out again. Tomorrow is a new day, life goes on and my favorite line of all "this too shall pass". Knowing who you are, is the beginning of loving who you are. So spend some time with you, it will be the most magical relationship in your life, only second to getting to know God!

Saved!

Lost!!
I am here
But where am i
I am scared and nervous
But I shall not cry
Where can I be?
What is keeping me here?
What is restricting me?
They say if you seek you, will find
Maybe I started seeking too late
Because all I feel is left behind
What is missing?

What did I miss
Am I missing a puzzle piece?
Did I miss my prince to kiss?
There is no fairytale
This is my reality
I am lost.
Am i?
I am growing more frightened
But I know I shouldn't cry
Is that a door?
Is someone trying to set me free?
How can I be trapped when I was lead here by me?
Should I open it?
Where will this lead me?
The room seems familiar
But now the walls seem to be closing in.
Is it me? Or is the room .....Spinning
Someone find me.. Please
I can't find my way
I want to give up, please rescue me.
How long have I been here?
How did I get here?
How do I get out of here?
I am screaming now
Can anyone hear me?
I am nervous, more than I was before
I want to go home
I don't want to be here anymore
I see no light, no compass to help me find my way
It's dark now
Is home this way?
The walls vanish
The sun must have gone down
I am terrified
Is it okay to cry now?
I am lost, I admit that now.
It's silent, I am the only sound.
How can I escape, how can I be free?

I am so so lost
Someone please find me!

He, who makes me...
I feel the faith
I can touch the air
I can finally see, and I can finally hear.
I've been down "that way",
and I've walked the dark road.
I've climbed the jagged mountain
and I have carried the heavy load.
I stand against all the evils, I was terrified of before.
I pray when I am scared, and I am not afraid anymore.
I honor the changes, and I feel the love
I thank him daily.
He, who is above
I have given him my heart, I have dedicated my soul
I pray when I am hurting, I pray when I am cold.
I didn't pray when I was running,
I didn't pray when I cried
I didn't pray when they betrayed me,
 I didn't pray when they lied.
I didn't pray when it was darkness,
 I didn't pray when I felt hate.
But one day he called for me,
and took all the anger from my plate.
I came to him broken; I came to him weak,
I came to him when I couldn't stand;
I came to him when I couldn't eat.
He dried my tears, he strengthened my back,
gave me a reason to believe
showed me the things I lacked.
I found him when I was lost,
or maybe it was he who found me.
Ever since, I have called for his help,
he has never denied me
I feel no worry; I cry no more, I see no hatred,

for it is he who allows it, it is he who i adore.
I am grateful to you now, more than ever before,
Thank you for blessing me every single day
this is a love poem to my lord and savior,
for it is he! And only he Who makes me feel.......
This way.

My true love poem
I was drowning in a sea
More like the Niagara Falls of misery
 Nonetheless...you saved me
How or when you did it, completely escapes me
Either way it still till this day. Amazes s me
First I lost all faith in love, people and finally my hope
Blaming everyone and everything
But never finding a solid scapegoat.
But from the bottom of disappear,
True beauty did magically appear.
More powerful than a thousand volts,
 And still as placid as a Childs prayer.
A majestic passion, something a simple mortal as myself
Has been programmed to fear.
But through all the hardships our love had proved to persevere.
Handicapped or doomed to repeat my mistakes
Until your faith in me, cleared my sight, and changed my fate,
It was your guidance, that educated me....
 And your grace that loved me so unconditionally.
You placed flowers in a place that used to sustain tears
You placed poetry where there once were fears
Grateful would be an understatement for the person you allowed me
to become
I understand I still have some growing to do, for your work is never
done
Constantly giving me gifts, even though
I can never repay you for that big one.
I knew your love then, when you sacrificed your only son.
I shall not disappoint you; I was not birthed in vain.

I can feel the beauty of the world in my heart
Whenever I think or even speak your name.
I am not sure what you have planned for me
I cannot see your ultimate vision
But I can promise to trust in you lord
And keep trying to honor you
With your permission.

Invincible
 Crying won't come,
tears won't move.
Trying won't win
but i can't afford to lose.
Victory seems faint
defeat seems quaint.
But i wont and i aint!
I see you achievement
i can smell you near
maybe it's the reason
i can't shed a tear
feet won't stand
hands can't become steady
can't see what's coming next
and yet somehow i am ready.
My body is weak, mind is confused
emotions unstable, and my heart feels used.
Ego is shot, pride is steady drifting away.
Words are still, never knowing what to say.
But what i do have is the love of Jesus
and the guidance of god
my faith is invincible
my lord your power is so powerful
to me.. it's incredible.

Life 101
If I stopped smiling
Then the frown would win

If I stopped laughing
Then the endless crying would begin.
If I stopped dreaming
Then my living fantasy would end.
If I stopped fighting for what I believed in
Well then, I was never meant to win!
If every day was perfect
Then no one would ever try.
Failure would be non-existent
Thus, success would be a lie.
Every day is a lesson and life is but a class.
If we weren't meant to get hurt and heal
Instead of flesh and bone
We would just be made of glass.
Struggle is a transition to prepare us for larger test.
So smile. Try and dream, and avoid circles filled with stress
Love every moment
And always remember you did your best.

Saved.

I didn't always understand faith. I didn't always understand how to pray. i didn't always know god was listening to me. I didn't always believe that god was real. I am no longer ashamed to admit this because we live and we learn. I have learned many things, and i have learned these things from god. Thank you lord.

You may be reading this and wondering one of two things, either you are a family member wondering what drugs Saduda is exploring or you are a friend laughing their head off stating "she will be back to her ol' Saduda-ish ways soon enough." i am glad to tell you all i am fine, sober, happy and completely sound of mind (if there is such a state for Saduda lol). I am saved, safe and completely sober. I feel....... so happy now that i am with god, I feel him all day inside me, above me and most of all beside me. Do you have any idea how greattttt!!! It feels to be in love with the lord????!!!! I am so blessed that god found me when he found me where he found me. I see insects flying around and they won't touch me, bite me, sting me, they just glide. I see weary people wondering around and they won't hurt me. I feel all the pain and the wrong that I have done and that has been done to me has been lifted and even forgotten.

I talked to god tonight, in the most beautiful place on the most beautiful night. He gave me peace; he gave me hope and completely restored my faith in everything. My heart that was broken and cold he healed. My fears he removed. My inhibitions no longer stifle me. I love you lord. I am writing this for no reason or credit i am just letting my hands write the thoughts god has placed in my head. i am happy that i am who i am today. I am blessed for meeting the people who i have met. I am stronger for the pain, and i am ready now. I just had some thoughts that needed to be expressed. Because what i felt tonight was something beautiful, thank you lord for allowing me to see. You saved me!

Life lessens.

Pointless!
You don't get it
There are certain things you say
And certain things you don't say
 No need to apologize
You already successfully pushed me away
You don't get it
There are ways you are home
Without actually being at home
You are always around but I am always alone
You don't get it
On paper we seem completely fine
But there are so many typos when reading between the lines
Commons in places there shouldn't be
Sentences missing periods, leaving thoughts
Incomplete, completely.
You don't get it.
Knock, knock who is there
No one, not here not anywhere

No one in the closet and no one under the bed
The sad part is that just went over your head
How do you love a poet?
 But don't know any of her poetry
How can you love me?
But don't love what I see myself be
I give you sonnets, epics of gold
Words so powerful, they break through a heart that
Is bitter and cold
You don't fucking get it
And thus you don't get me
I am reading the lining of my heart and
Still don't hear me.
You don't get me, you don't understand the way I flow
I end with a plea.
Learn me, or just please let me go.

Bipolar.
Not sure if I am getting pissesd off
or just pissed on.
 I love you , yet loving you is starting to sound so wrong
You spark these emotions,
Only you can find in me
It looks like love but feels like jealousy.
Your ability to create insecurities
shaped us into something... ugly
An unconditional love
Colored in uncertainty
Standing behind envy
While drowned in immaturity.
Trapped in a love that bears my soul
You make me hot with anger
But treat me so cold
You're such a dick!
 See what you make me do
I feel so abusive when I am with you.
Are you battered, are you soar
Am I a bitch if I don't love you anymore?

This is purely physical for me,
 That would make you my whore
Don't be offended, it's a compliment baby
Because you are my highest level of ecstasy
Every time you enter me
I feel a touch of something heavenly
This is when I feel my weakest
And there I see you; I'm trapped in my quivering body
Wait for it, I'll start to resent you.
Get away from me
But please baby, don't leave
I only hate you when you're here
When you're gone I can't breathe,
It's not you it's me, it's not you it's me.
I am in capable of staying happy,
It's why I seek pain again and again
I am... Empty. Nothing within
I am caged within myself
There is nothing wrong with me
Melancholy is my best friend.

You win!
I don't want to argue,
and i am not prepared to fight.
I really want to watch a scary movie
and hold you throughout the night.
I just want to wake up
with no makeup
make you pancakes
and eggs sunny side up.
I really don't have the energy
to scream anymore
I want to kiss you and listen to you sleep
not the sound of breaking dishes and slamming of doors.
I want to read you poetry
since they are all about you

i want us to just be beautiful
i really don't want to argue.

Never ever after.
Don't you just get bored waiting for the happy ending?
Or maybe that's just me,
It's so hard being patient
Waiting For something
You may or may not see.
I am damsel but I am not in distress!
Maybe that's why Charming ...
Hasn't courted me just yet
Should I be panting?
Hand over my forehead
Waiting for the handsome prince,
To rescue me?
Not to sound like Ms. Independent
But...I have never been good at resuming vulnerability
I'm impatient, thus I have stopped waiting
Instead, i snuck out the back door while
My heart and mind were deliberating
I have to confess, it was quite liberating!
Single seemed so pathetic, from a distance
One is the loneliest number
Convinced me
I admit this.
But now after all the drama,
 cheating, lying and make up nights
The drinking, partying, and text messaged fights
The ignored calls, the absent lover,
the infidelity blamed one another
Between cursing you and hating myself..
 Once more forgiving,
While tarnishing my mental health
I clean up the broken dishes and
stare at the holes in the walls
As I wonder is any of this worth it at all.
You spend your whole life

trying to fill what we assume is a void
Sadly once you find it
You're either home alone waiting,
 or overcrowded and annoyed.
This isn't true for everyone; some make a way to co exists.
And I salute those who find ways to make blankets of all the bullshit
To the blind I sound bitter, to the jaded I'm just a little one sided
I can't front this happily ever after thing
Always left me feeling emotionally divided.
Trust me..I've tried it.
Truth is........Picket fences coil in bad weather conditions
Two and half kids, shit on carpets causes drinking additions.
I love cooking but i hate doing the dishes
And I could puke at the thought,
Of scrubbing floors, while he's out
Brainwashing his next mistress.
I laugh at the idea, most times I frown
Imagine...Being his mother, wife, bed room slut,
But more often, his clown.
So I left the tallest tower,
 i pretended my glass slipper didn't fit.
I called Romeo before I took that poison
Gave the wizard the finger and said
Fuck this shit!
I was happy long before the ever after
I am going to have a drink with the big bad wolf
Tell prince charming,
I will shoot him a text
Very ever after.

The ex.
He treats love like meaningless game
and this i couldn't see
That's why my inner voice abandoned me.
Now I'm comatosed since removing the IV
I never knew it was this
Valuable to me.
Never felt so used?

No pride in how swiftly I have succumbed
He was enjoying the benefits
While I'm out there calling him the one.
He was my ultimate heartache
 and that i didn't believe
This was around the time
 my common since decided to leave
I know what i know and that is, he loves me.
 I would say this repeatedly as i grieve.
No one could even begin to convince me
That the person i was loving,
was the very reason I was so unhappy.
I just wanted to be happy.
He is the ultimate manipulator,
but it was I Who brain washed poor little me.
All these years pretending,
that he was more than giggles in my love history
I was the idiot who let him echo inside me.
Our happiest days quickly becoming a hazy blur
Through the smoke we saw the truth about each other.
That what was once there, was there no more
These are only memories that we cherish
It's the past we adore
Those feeling were questions we didn't need to answer
Giving into stale emotions, touches we will regret after.
Always pulling me into your time machine,
So we can relive our past, me living in a dream
You already fully aware it wouldn't last.
Too selfish to just be honest with me
You made it clear that you didn't love me; I was too arrogant to see
And I was in love with the idea of what we should be.
You only want me when I'm gone; you only need me to need you.
It's my heart break that beckons, and my tears that lead you.
You never had any intention of taking me seriously
You were just luring me repeatedly, to use me for sex.
Spoiler alert, that's usually to motive of the ex.

Unfair affair.
I'm debating over giving him my heart.
But I am a little weary
I mean he isn't even single, yet
And that my friend is scary.
To become a mistress
When I am clearly so much more
It's wrong I know, and you're ashamed I'm sure
But with him it's almost worth it
Echoes of our love seem absolutely perfect.
I am his princess, and he most defiantly is my prince.
Like those weekends we don't leave the house
Just for instance.
But now he is planning baby showers.
And it's not with me.
Crying on the inside while pretending to be happy.
So hard to admit I am just your mistress, still.
It's so hard to believe that our fairytale wasn't real
Spending the entire summer broken hearted
Was the realest thing you ever made me feel.
But when the rain comes, and our song is playing
I can feel your heart beating inside me,
As I breathe the words you were always saying.
My dreams are smothered in visions of you.
I watch nervously.
At the tormenting reality of you and me
Hoping this time when it ends, it ends differently.
An ending without pain and misery.
One where I am forever yours and you are not always leaving me.
As magical as our fairytale used to be
It's over now.
And your happily ever after
Doesn't end with me.

Just her... Not me.
I need you to touch me and say I am better than her
Give me those looks that

make your relationship ..just a blur
I need you to hold me tight, even after 6am
I need you to introduce me as your lover,
not a co-worker or friend.
I need to feel your hand on mine,
 in public during the day
I want you to notice me and
 not just turn the other way.
I want to call your home, and you actually answer
I need you to make me feel like I am better than her.
I imagine she is nothing like me
Does she make you smile, are you truly happy.
Does she admire you while you sleep?
Trace your face, and play our song on repeat.
Cherish our moments no matter how short, their always fun
Relive them over and over, until you give me new ones.
Never able to grasp what he can see in her
Everything is I know is telling me we belong together
I bet she can't love you like me?
Can she?
That's why He is leaving her,
 Isn't he?
He doesn't love her, he can only love me.
I imagine the day that I become the wife
And I experience the days where
you don't come home at night
Our days are spent arguing
 over these unanswered calls
As I give my friends unbelievable excuses
 for the holes in our walls.
I needed so badly to feel better than her,
 back when I was that unidentified caller
But her life is miserable, and I was the one hurting her.
See karma is real, and more spiteful
Than I imagined it would be.
I thought if we traded places
He would never cheat on me.
The truth is, it's a cycle, and he just recycled me.

If you are the mistress, and you are dying to be the wife
Don't worry sweetheart, soon you will have her exact life.
See, at some point we all believe we can change a man
I can stop him from cheating, I just know I can.
I can make him happy, if he was only with me.
He will be different one day they will see!
I am sorry to tell you, we have all been fooled to believe
The words that secure our sanity until the day he leaves.
Just her, not me. Just her, not me!

Life lesson number 13
No one ever warned me
Just how convincing kids can be
How quickly friends can turn on you
Watching the ones you trust the most,
 Soon become enemies
You keep them so close,
Unaware, They are plotting your demise
Covering secrets with smiles, and lies with other lies.
But you, the oh so trusting
 never seeing their true form.
Doings things they tell you are right
Finding yourself in places you know are wrong
Until that one day, when the real you is completely erased
Strings embed in your backbone
while a mindless puppet takes your place
So blindly you are lead, by our pressuring peers
Your puppet master retires.
Leaving you alone, with all your regrets and tears.

Not everything that is good for them, will be good for you
Not everything they try, means you have to ..too
Not everyone who claims to be your friend
Is who they lead you to believe.
Lesson number 13.
When you feel out of place
That's the best time to leave.

Life lesson number 21
It's when you accept you messed up
When the pain hurts the most
That knowledge that you destroyed something
That thing that once allowed you to brag and boast
You're very aware of what you have done
Excuses given all in the name of fun.
The mistakes you both have made
Watching the memories collapse but still,
reminiscing as they fade.
The lies you told seemed appropriate at the time
But here you are, standing 5 inches tall,
red in face as they unfold.
Only you and I know
You being my heart, and I being my soul.
Those acts of lust
Often make our hearts turn cold.
No one means for anyone to get hurt
No one plans to devastate the one person they love most
There are those moments in-between,
where the love you are betraying
Surfaces, but says nothing.
It simply stares as you throw it all away
You part your lips but have no words to say.
There it warns you, and quickly backs away.
I've given parts of myself that I should not
I knew it was wrong, but I was too selfish to stop
I am sorry if I harmed you.
I am sorry if you hate me now
I am sorry if you feel used
I am sorry if I let you down.
I am so sorry I gave your love to another.
Life lesson number 21
Be faithful to each other.

Life lesson no. 26
So I will smile a little less
I will pray these temptations digress
I will cope with the acceptance
And the reality of my interest.
I will not fulfill my passion.
Justifiable emotions
UN justifiable reactions
Thirst and hunger
Lead to oh so fatal attractions
He cannot belong to me
I must not try to make it so
Breathe in deeply
And simply let him go.
The courtship, oh what potential it showed
The conflicting situation,
Oh what grief it bestowed,
To whom it is given
Is not to whom it is owed
Still, I will not fulfill my passion
The burden, deceitful beauty
Chemical reaction, reacting to the attraction,
Instinctively.
There! Deep within the fairytale
Lies the foe
Educating the spirit, on what it didn't want to know.
Enter stage left, the tainted Romeo
The lyrically gifted, chiseled charming prince
Guarded by an already white picket fence.
I was born spoiled, which means, I gotta get it some how
Go away conscience, leave me moral
I refuse to be Nobel,
I want what I want and I want it now!!
Come back... he said,
To those thoughts... in back of your head
She will cry
He, will always be forced to lie
And You ! You? Will die a little more each day inside.

            M.E.   84

There will be rules which only you must abide.
You will suffer neglect and a new level of emotional stress
If you accept... the role as his.. Mistress.
Dear god is this a cruel test.
No,
This is simply...life lesson number 26.

Dear Dreamer.
In dreams we find.. Sprinkles and glitter
From that optimistic child we left behind.
In dreams we see
Smaller yet braver versions of you and me
In dreams we hear
The whispers that remind us
we can achieve anything and we can go anywhere
In dreams we feel
The textures of the sky, as clouds and rain peddles of surreal.
Within our dreams lies the person we were destine to be
So close your eyes and dream,
and stop wasting time listening to me!

Life lessons.

Throughout my life I had been blessed to learn some very valuable lessons. I have been lucky enough to learn things that regardless of how badly they hurt they didn't kill me. I have lived a life full of mistakes, heart aches and bad decisions but no regrets. In life you will do what feels right at the time, rarely do we think of tomorrow. I remember falling in love with a married man. I remember choosing a man's love over the love of my friends. I remember letting people in my home who betrayed me. I remember a lot of horrible things I have done and I have had done to me. But I don't remember being ashamed of my past. The beautiful thing about life's lessons is you actually learn something from it. You can take something from it that will not only teach you, but give you a story to educate others. They key is to go forward! Change what needs to be changed and believe in progress. You can't do this when you are surrounded by self-doubt and negative thinkers. I have been cleaning my house a lot lately, "metaphor", I have been cleansing myself of the people and things that are no good for me or my home....

Lately i have been learning more and more about real life and all its struggles. I am tired of the back stabbing, the two faced people and the phonies, the malicious actions that have left me with no benefits. Lately I have been more aware that I am one of a kind, and will often be taken for granted. I determine my self-worth, but others determine what I am worth by my actions.

So I stopped sitting around waiting for someone to help me, or hand me anything. Instead I decided to leave my mark on the world. If you want to get anything you must do it yourself. Lately i have been learning that people will only do what is best for them, not caring who it hurts in the process, not all but some people.

I am no fool, i was never one to allow a person to take advantage of me and yet it happens to us all. People will do what you allow them to do to you. No one knows you are hurting if you don't make a sound. I used to be the super hero, fix everyone's problems, look past the flaws, try and save the day, and patiently wait around for someone I love to start doing right by me. Yes i learned the hard way that you can't change someone or force them to respect you. Regardless of how much energy you exert, there is no guarantee people will treat you the way you treat them. My grandfather taught me many things in my life, before he went to heaven, for example: how to shuffle cards like a pro, how to play spades like a King, and how to NOT change a tire and to let my smile and femininity do it for me (lol). But the one thing that sticks out in my mind the most is .. You cannot change anyone but yourself. I can try and try until I am sick to my stomach to change a person or make them see their ways, but i would only be wasting my time. Selective vision is common among people nowadays; we only see what we want to see, even in the mirror. I have allowed many people to hurt me waiting on them to change, soon i learned that it will never happen so i finally got up and walked away, thankfully never looking back. ONCE I AM GONE, I AM GONE.

Now i am a strong believer in Two powerful forces, God and Karma.

M.E.   86

Karma is what keeps me from seeking revenge on those who have caused me harm (we are not talking about self-defense, I am all for that). I learned that people will always do what is best for themselves and completely disregard the feelings of others. We live in a world where you live and you learn. You get what you give. This is why we must let things go and learn from them. Instead of stressing yourself over a past you cant change embrace it. Take those bruises that life has given you and wear them with pride. People who hurt you will one day see the wrong of their ways, either way they are not your problem. You give them too much power by obsessing over the things they have done. Someone abandon you when you needed them the most they did you a favor. I am always excited when I reach my rock bottom to see how much people really care and how loved I truly am. The smaller your circle gets the further you go. People who do not support you at your worst don't deserve you at your best. They are only going to pull you down later.

I will not allow those who don't want to prosper to hold me back. I will not allow the negative energy of others to destroy my smile. I am destined for greatness and I will not allow anyone or anything to make me question myself. I know I try hard, hell i work hella hard, two jobs for as long as I can remember. I fight for what i love and defend the ones I love by all means. I go out of my way to help people and i will never change that for anyone. I love continuing to try to do the right thing. You don't have to believe a word I said, in fact you can lie to yourself and say these are not raw facts, but it wouldn't change anything. Because I have learned so much from this book, from the words I myself have written about myself. Remember your past can be a lot of things but it can never be your present. I have learned one very important lesson, Love who you are. You can't change anyone but yourself, so love yourself more than you love anyone else.

Part five: Memory lane

Something's missing
There were trees
But no leaves

Shoes but not laces
People with no faces.
Something's missing.
Everything was wrong
Short was long
Hot was cold
New was old.
Something's missing.
Well at least somebody's listening.
Then I looked over to see that
You weren't standing beside me.
I didn't want to cry but my tears kept insisting
in my eyes the world was wrong,
but in reality you were the only thing missing.

Ghetto fairytale

When they met
There was no love at first sight
He thought she had a fatty
She thought his game was tight.
No poetic catch lines
Just jokes and drinks
He made her laugh
She made him think
There were no vows
No romantic walks
No deep and meaningful looks
No long and boring talks
Some arguments
And a couple of petty fights
A little mix of jealousy
Topped with a lot of passionate nights
He cheated, she cried.
She confronted, and he lied.
Not every day was easy
Some nights were cold
Many live in a ghetto fairytale
WILL YOU ADMIT WHEN YOUR STORY IS TOLD?

M.E.

Bitter taste.
Yuck!
The memories you left behind
With Irreversible damage you did to my mind
The joy you stole from my day
The three little big words, you'd never actually say.
The laughter you banded from this home
The crying girl you always left alone
The countless burses, your feet left on my heart.
The love you ruined, but weren't part of from the start.
It's so sour, I can't remember the sweet.
As I recall this love was
Painful, crazy, Dramatic, exhausting and emotionally oblique.
This bitter taste you left was everything
Everything except sweet!

The night.
Sweetest man in the world,
A virgin but a very bright girl
everything he said she loved, and then it was hand in glove.
It was a night both would remember,
it was a rainy day in cold December
not caring she only met him today,
Not knowing as he kissed her
He took her purity away,
Moves were made, I love you was said
Yet as they rolled across the bed
before the night was through
She pushed out the words I love you
morning had now come and both had had their fun
but where was her Romeo, where did he go?
She opened her eyes and lifted her head
A rose on the pillow, a letter on the bed, she opened as it read
"In the body I did proceed a little white lie is all you need,

To open your heart to a man of steel, even now wishing my presence
you could fell.
One such as yourself I gave to you what I gave to no one else
a gift you can take to your health
because you treated me as if you were 100 maids
well my gift to you is aids....
oh and in case you didn't get my name, I never wanted yours so who is
to blame?"
She closed her eyes and began to cry
rubbed her stomach and said
"I guess both baby and I must die."

The human violin.
Rhythm dances through the mind
A sound which is dangerously one of a kind
With each stroke of a string
it's like a song which is too beautiful to sing
A rough stroke brings it a streak
a gentle stroke makes its sound so unique
A humming whisper when it's notes are played
A painful withdrawal when its sound shall fade
The human violin
With string for a heart
And rhythm for a soul,
When playing it's playing... listen
For it's a story to be told.
And when its silence seems to begin
It smiles art!
It ends a sin
suddenly, its eyes stare with a great force
beware: "*If this violin be too admired*
its beauty be lost."

Broken
Realization, it was all based on a lie.
She compressed her tears struggling not to cry.

An invisible knife, cutting her heart straight from her chest
She loved him as much as she could, she gave him her best.
So terrified he would leave,
She loved him more than she loved herself, if you can believe.
He simply said he just didn't feel the same.
Afterwards it burned so greatly just to speak his name
It seemed so recent, the happiness they shared
The days she laughed, the days he cared.
Feeling incomplete too hurt to smile, too sad to eat.
Death was too dramatic, suicide full of shame
Cutting herself felt like nothing, his absence was the only pain.
Two pills and two shots.. how quickly Reality fades.
"is this my fault?" as she cries, in the spot where he once laid.
Liquor makes it easier to deal.
The pills make it harder to feel
Pictures of him everywhere, she needs another drink
How many pills is that?
More liquor …less think
Memories return.. It's over ..but Why?
Stop it eyes, don't do that! Don't cry.
She finished the bottles
Just trying to forget him
Make his memory go away
Feeling Sleepy now
Rest your eyes, Lay down
Tomorrow will be okay.
Tomorrow will make everything go away.

Downfall
As her heart descents
 Her temperature rises
Its then she cries
And that's when she realizes
There is no more him
There is no more forever
Her world shatters around her
Yet she continuously struggles to keep it together
 the tears are already there

Her cheeks still moist with a failed love
From a man who doesn't care.
A connection so distant, it's closer to non-existent
Still not ready to release him
She clings to all she knows
Her heart still convincing her he'll return..
But.... there he goes.

I'd rather
I'd rather know life was a single day long
Than to know tomorrow you'd be gone.
I'd rather live life gasping for air.
If it meant you'd always be there.
I'd rather hear screams every hour of my day
Than to miss a single word you say.
I'd rather live in shame and poverty
If it meant you'd still love me.
I'd rather continue life in a coma,
If I could still smell your aroma
I'd rather fight every war in history
Than to put you through any misery.
I'd rather be blind and completely insane.
Than to watch you go through any pain.
I'd rather be numb from head to toe.
Than to feel your arms let me go.
I'd rather be made of stone, than for you to ever leave me alone.
I'd rather feel completely empty, than to imagine you don't love me.
I'd rather believe my nightmare will come true.
Than for you to think I don't believe in you
I'd rather never see another day
If there love we have went away.
There is nothing I wouldn't do for you
Nowhere I wouldn't go for you
There is everything I want to give you.
Even if death told me to stop loving you
Or my soul he'd gather
I'd tell him with my last breath

I'd rather.

History.
These years we call him the man
But when Trying to escape, they hit more than just your hand
Martin Luther King, he had a dream
They took that dream and made us cry
We'd fight back, but then we had to die.
What or who gave you the right
To beat us from day till night
To rape us in tainted grass.
To treat us no better than trash
They can't break us, but they sure can try
Take our, children , our husbands, our lives.
But they will never get our pride.
No one should ever feel this much pain
No human should ever sleep in the rain.
As a result what have you learned?
What ..tell me.. what have you earned?
Nothing that you can show.
Why you even did it, you still don't know
Slavery, segregation, hanging, AND OH YEA rape
And they call us the COLORED race.
There is nothing you can say to change it
You WONT say *sorry*
AND You can't change history.
What can you do?
you can't take it back
A PLETHERA OF hatred and pain
Just because I'm black!
Well, there AINT enough apologies
In the world
To change the mind of this little girl!
And that my friend is HISTORY!

Memory lane.

I was between the age of 12 and 15 for all of these poems. I didn't know I was gifted, I didn't know i was an instrument. I knew that when I wrote for whatever reason I felt better. I knew that I love the expression I received when people found out I was a poet. I got high off the disbelief in their eyes when they learned the "black girl writes". I remember being the only black girl in my class many times in my life, always feeling out of place because of my race, but never because of my intelligence. I have been treated unfairly for no other than the color of my skin. I could say "shut up" to a coworker and immediately I am a threat, and another girl of a different race could say "shut up" to a coworker and it's a joke. I have been treated unfairly more times than I can count and I am mature enough now to say it won't stop. Even when I make a respectable name for myself as a writer I will always be seen as black first and writer second.
I am more than a color. I am more than a sex. I am vision embodied. I am lyrics to a song that has yet to be written. I have been writing since I was 5 years old. Before my brain could properly spell I was trying to use words that felt right but had no meaning to me. I was expressing feelings I hadn't even felt yet. Explain that? I have poetry inside of me that needs to be set free, before I could even understand it was dying to get out. Now this is it! My book! My story! My pain , my happiness. My emotions are explained in poetical definition.

These last two poems are for my Older Sister Ife and Grandfather who have both passed on. I am not good with poems about the deceased. But these two are significant to my life in such a way I needed to write these for them both.

Family affair. (to Ife my sister)
I want to understand
I really wanna get it!
The shoe is on my foot
But I am pretending I can't fit it
The emotion is confusing
Overwhelming at the least
I am fighting a nightmare

But I am losing against this beast!
Give her back to me.

Losing a sister
Feels so so wrong
I am known for my logic
Yet it's hard to understand she's gone
I sleep now
With very little to dream about
I want the pain to go away
But my heart won't let it out
Why mine? Is what I can't figure out!
This family is supposed to be invincible
Indestructible, incapable of defeat.
So imagine my confusion
When the crying would not cease.

When losing someone so vital,
Asking someone you love to rest in peace.
Asking you to leave me, is a favor I can't beseech.
Maybe holding on is just selfish of me.

We stick together,
Stronger than any tribe
Having our issues and problems
But handled those inside

They are more than just my family
They are my entire world
Now it's struggling to recover
After losing one of its baby girls.

The tears will be great
The lost is already dire
The unity will be poetic
But the love will hold the most power.

I am trying to grasp it

To believe what they are telling me
But I refuse to accept
We've lost such a beautiful member
Of such a strong family.

Writer's block.

There's never been a day where "Sabuda"
Had nothing to say.
Never been a moment, where a poem wouldn't just flow.
Where you'd ask me to write one and I'd say no.
Yet I've never known such a lost.
when writers block came at the ultimate cost.
To freeze all the words I need to say
To comfort grandma and tell her it will be okay.
Remind her that he is in a better place.
And that it's only sad
Because, tomorrow we can't see his face.
Crying is natural so let your tears flow.
It's okay to be emotional and let your feelings show.
Because he was perfect, truly carved from diamonds and gold.
Therefore no man will ever fit his mold
He was many things, among are a few.
A spades master, a card trickster, a Pac man king
And a bowler that could knock down anything, a father, a pop-pop
and truly my best friend, I could confide in you always, easing my
pain before I even begin.
I am trying to convince myself that this isn't real
That this pain that I am feeling
I don't really feel.
If you didn't know him, I am sorry for you
There was nothing he couldn't fix, or even try to.
Nothing he couldn't build, no game he couldn't defeat
No pain he couldn't heal, no butter pecan he wouldn't eat.
I am grateful to have known granddaddy so well.
To have him never pronounce my name correctly,
But to always catch me when I fell.

M.E.   96

To have him present in my life, to father my aunts and make grandma his wife.
I learned today, why writers block exist.
Mine was the result of an overwhelming pain
Of losing someone I will dearly miss.
As hard as this poem was, its only you who could get me through this.

Love sabuda to my one and only grand daddy.
To grandma
From Saduda with love

If God has blessed me to be published and spread my words, I know that there was a divine reason I felt the pain that I felt when I wrote them. I know that by being blessed with this gift of expression through poetry I have to help others that suffer .By sharing my poems others will understand they are not the only ones and that hurt and there is a reason for it all. Regardless if you see the reason today or tomorrow or years later there is a reason. Trust in Him; Trust that he is either making you stronger to strengthen others, educating you so that you can educate others. Or training you to be the person who made you to be. The happiness we as people have experienced is used to help us work hard to achieve that happiness once more. If you let God in your life, it help you reach that happiness now and for eternity. I have been writing poetry for as long as I can remember and it has always helped me to heal. I was able to write it down, record it and save it. All of my poems allowed me to learn and in some cases I have touched others. I am so grateful for my poetry because on many occasions it has saved my life in more ways than one. If anyone ever reads this book and it helps them to understand any questions they may have had about love, friendship or just need to know someone knows how you feel. It's me. If ever need someone to see things from your perspective it's me. If you ever need someone to help you when no one seems to know what to do, well that is Gods area but feel free to read the book anyway. Lol.

Thank you!!!!!!

Thank you Lord for everything you have allowed me to survive and learn. Thank you GOD for giving me the gift of poetry at such a young age. Thank you Mommie for always believing in me and telling me I am your favorite, oopps, that was a secret. For being the strongest, smartest and funniest woman I know. I am grateful for every single moment I share with you! Thank you to my sister Yasmine, for listening to all my rough drafts and poems I wrote on napkins. Thank you Ms. Hooper for teaching me more than just 10th grade English, and always seeing more in me than I was capable of seeing in myself. Thank you Naima for supporting me in more ways than one! Thank you Nephew for bringing a new type of joy to my life. Thank you Afalalu my sister for loving me unconditionally and financially. Thank you Kendell Hollins for always telling me how great you think I am, for educating me every chance you get, for being you when I need you most. I love you!

Thank you to My last two jobs I worked that inspired me to finish my book and return to school, so no one else will take advantage of me. Thank you to my family who ask me every other day where's the book! Thank you Mazi for all the poetry you listened to and helped perfect! Thank you to my other older brother who was reading my poetry in secret but still paid me a compliment when I began to doubt myself. Thank you to all the heart breakers, all the disappointments, all the pain and love. Thank you to those I have missed!

Thank you to all my readers I hope these words can help you the way they helped me!
Feel free to contact me.
Sadudao@gmail.com

www.ingramcontent.com/pod-product-compliance
Lightning Source LLC
Chambersburg PA
CBHW051735040426
42447CB00008B/1147